NO TRUSTPASSING

HOOD & FACE 1

Join Us on Social Media

The Legit Styles

The Legit Styles

Legit Styles Publishing

NO TRUSTPASSING!

EVERYTHING BEGINS WITH TRUST!
WITHOUT IT THERE IS NO US!
WITHOUT IT THERE IS NO LOVE!
TRUST HOLDS EVERYTHING TOGETHER
IT ERASES DOUBT AND MAKES SURE ALL STORMS ARE
WEATHERED
BELIEVING IN TRUST ENABLES RELATIONSHIPS TO GROW
IT TURNS ARGUMENTS INTO CONVERSATIONS ALLOWING
LOVE TO FLOW!
SO LET TRUST LEAD US, GUIDING OUR LIVES
TURNING OUR CLOUDY DAYS INTO SUNSHINE
AND OUR DULL NIGHTS INTO STAR FILLED SKIES
ALWAYS SHOWING US THE TRUTH ABOUT TRUST
WHEN EVER WE FEEL WEAK LET TRUST STRENGTHEN US
AND NEVER FORGET EVERYTHING BEGINS WITH TRUST
WITHOUT IT THERE IS NO US!
WITHOUT IT THERE IS NO LOVE!
TRUST IS A KEY ELEMENT IN OUR EVERYDAY LIVES!

A poem by FACE 1

Face 1
SPECIAL DEDICATION

THIS RIGHT HERE IS DEDICATED TO THREE VERY SPECIAL, IMPORTANT, AND LOVED PEOPLE IN MY LIFE! MR. EDDIE PACE, DARRYL TITTLE AND NA'IL DOWNING. FAMILY, I SEND MY LOVE, MY HOPE AND MY FAITH THAT THE MAN UPSTAIRS WILL CONTINUE HIS HOLD ON YOU AS YOU ALL CONTINUE ON THE JOURNEY AHEAD. UNDERS-TAND AND KNOW THAT THE FIGHT HAS JUST BEGUN. WITH EVERYDAY THAT PASSES, WE ALL ARE CLOSER TO BEING BACK TOGETHER AGAIN AND TRUST AND BELIEVE THAT IT WILL DEFINITELY HAPPEN AGAIN!

EDDIE- IT'S BEEN A LONG TIME; RELATIVE YOU ARE SO GREATLY MISSED.

DARRYL- THE WORLD YOU LIVED IN WASN'T READY FOR YOU AT THE TIME. JUST GIVE THEM TIME, THEY WILL FINALLY CATCH UP AND OH YEAH, CONTINUE TO STAND ON YOUR OWN SQUARE IT WILL PAY OFF IN THE END.

NA'IL- HEAR ME OUT AND HEAR ME GOOD! SOMETIMES HARSH THINGS HAPPEN TO THE GREAT ONES. IT'S UP TO US TO MAKE THE BEST OUT OF THAT HARSH SITUATION. LI'L RELLY KEEP YOUR HEAD UP AND CHEST OUT! STAY GROUND-ED, PRAYERED UP AND THE REST WILL PAVE ITS OWN WAY!

TO MS WILLIAMS, THANK YOU FOR YOUR HARD WORK, YOUR UNSEEN WORK, AND YOUR DILIGENT WORK. WITHOUT IT THIS PROJECT WOULD HAVE NEVER SEEN THE LIGHT OF DAY....

TO MY DAUGHTERS:

KHIYA, UAWNDRENÈ, AND AUNJAHLI

You are my sun, my breath, and my life! L.U.T.I.G!

To my loved ones behind the wall, Clydieus you've always been my favorite Li'l relative and I got the kite you sent. I see you've grown up! E Lil' Eric, get it right I'm going to need you nephew. Lil' Bam and Baby Bam, ya boy been checking up on y'all. Stay strong! Bud Luv and Baby Bud, L's Clee-Bone, Don Diego and Lil' Matt Bo Bo, had to say what's up to some real nigga's. Monkey "D", T-Way, Lil' Way, Tiny Hatt, Lil' Duece, Fatal, Kendu, V-Bone, T-Mighty, J-Fox, Blackout, Shoe Baby, Herman, Harv Nutty, Suga Shaft, Nadia, and Paul-Paul. What it do Tiny Lon. My O.G.'s that paved the way and the young homies that keep it paved. Y.P.'s, Termites, M.S.O.G.'s, Green Demons, MGK, Clack Unit and Tha Young Lynch Mob. We gotta find a way, until then keep pushin'.

R.I.P. Grandpa Poppa and Grandma Kareemah, Thelma, Big Earl, Izola (AKA) Leggs, Marshi and Lil' Mike, I miss you all...Uncle Larry, Aunt Mary, Conrad, Tranell, Uncle Johnny, Redd, Brenda Freeman, Bubba Cheeks, Chach, Lil' Doodie, D-Lo, Lil' Wicked, Demaj, Kareeb Jackson, Billy Vennible, Bank Bootie, Jenable, and Lil' Bandit! You all are never forgotten and continue to be missed!

To the mothers of my daughters, Patrice, Melisha and Kenya thank you for helping me create three beautiful angels! Aunty Sharon I'm so proud of you. You came up from the ground up. Lil' Face keep doin you! I don't know where I would be without you. Sam Bam, I've learned so much from you and you didn't even know it. Wydell, I love you, boy! Darius, when I was little I thought you invented the hustle game (lol) Butch, you've been around since the beginning. Bezo, B-Note and Face. Samir, Lil' Dirty Red, Eric B, Buincy, Joe Babe, Bee Doubles, Mikey Dred, Pimpin Marv, Tear Bear, T-White 59/50, My young nigga Mar-Mar, KB, Roni Ron, what it do? Victor and to my nigga Baby Wood, we on now! Pookie, remember Mt. Miguel? Cash and Meech, I told y'all. Welcome home Jinx, Brimlin, and Black Charlie. Now make it count ridahs!! Boobster, stay focused I'm almost there. Fetti Mack, Diego to Denver. Byron "CEO" Grey, I appreciate you bringing my vision to the eyes of the world! You won't regret it! Nutty, stay on your grind. I see you proving a lot of people wrong. Lil' Hatt and Baby Hatt, your boy got his eyes on you, what's popping? Tish Babe, I love you big sis, Bookie, Kee Kee, Cat Daddy, Rashonda, Mickey, Took Nasty, Eesh, Shema, Trelly, Tarik, Bill Bill, Khalid, Wahleed, Lil' Zack, Waheed, Poopie, Reece, Rahim, Marcell, Jaque, "FREAKA H20", Cee Cee, Adena, Tiyanna, and to my brother Bashieff, one dream lived a few more to go. Last but definitely not least, my Victorville (1) Homies, B-lazy, K-Rock, Smoke, Kobra Loko, Bop, Big Zulu, Lil' T-Bo Bo, JaBaar, G-Wayne, Ooh-Wee (R.I.P.) Bandit, Al Capone, E-Rock, Nate Rell Rule, Profit and to my Baby Bro D-Good, you pushed me and look what happened!!!!! Yeah dat! We are nothing without the homegirls! Check out Endangered Species coming soon.

With that being said, and until the next time.

Strength -n- Love

Diego's Finest

P.S. If I forgot you please don't fault me, send me a letter or an email and I promise to bless you on the next run! 100...

Hood's Shout Outs

First and foremost, I have to thank God for making all of this possible. Without him none of this would be. I would like to thank my family and close friends, my wife Ebony, Kim B, Pat Mya and the rest of the crew for your tips and pointers along the way. Big shout out and rest in Peace to the Soul of my QUEEN my MOTHER "GLORIA ", My Pops, Lil' Brah "TY", Big brah "WALLY", My sister's Tonya and Kay-Kay, niece and all my nephews coming up. Big shout out to my Jersey homies, "SUWU if you bangin'", my NY homies, and My B-More Homies much love. Big shout out to the Mid-West homies that showed love, all the West Coast niggas that been there for me. Lil' Macky, G, Bless, Good, Day-Day, Big Slim, Snap G, Hump, Wax-A-Don a real nigga and author of "REPO MAN", Trigga, My St. Louis nigga S. Dot, Bang, all the real nigga's doing their time in Leavenworth USP. The most respect to my homie, my friend and business partner FACE 1. Much love my nigga, we did this mo' fucker...Support the movement, this is far from over and we are on the rise. Big Up's to my Texas homies Big B's to you nigga's. Be on the lookout for that Endangered Species, Full Circle, Chess Not Checkers 1, 2, 3, Power Of The Pussy, RUN, also The H.0.0.D movement is on the way, gotta give back to them kids, that A.C.H.O clothing line is popping as well. Jersey City stand up, San Diego Standup, Wattz Stand up. California to Jersey Love. Do your time in the right mind and always be a Man of Influence! God Bless.

Chapter One
Chance

"Do you have anything you want to say before you're sentenced, Mr. Hood?" the pink, pale faced judge asked before he gave me my time.

I had to laugh to myself before I said, "Nah I'm good. Y'all gonna give me what y'all think it is I deserve anyway. So go ahead and do what you do."

My attorney kicked my foot before I sat down. *What the fuck was she mad about? She got twenty Gs out of me so she should be all smiles.*

"Mr. Hood, I hereby sentence you to one hundred and twenty months in a federal penitentiary. Get outta my courtroom!"

Bang! Bang! Bang!

NINE YEARS LATER...

Oh shit. When I opened my eyes I instantly became upset. Looking at my G-shock wristwatch it read 3:36 a.m.

"Fuck," I hissed as I tried to get comfortable.

Sleep had been hard to come around but for good reason. I was going home in seventy-two hours. Yep, this shit was finally over. Nine funky ass years. That was 3,285 days in the Federal system. *Let me get up and watch some TV.* I thought to myself. *Yeah that's what I'll do...*

1

TWO HOURS LATER...

It was about time this cracker ass C.O. turned the lights on. I'm ready to get the fuck out of this cell. Not to mention, my cellie, Nu'voe was on the top bunk farting up a storm. He had the room smelling like baby shit. That was my nigga though, and it was going to hurt to leave him behind in a few days. In fourteen more months he'd be out and we could touch base on the street.

After I brushed my teeth and washed up, I decided to wake my nigga up. If I didn't, he'd sleep until lunch.

"Yo, celly!" I yelled, while pushing his leg.

Finally coming to, he looked around, all ugly in the face.

"What time is it, homie?" he asked.

"Get ya ass up nigga. The door 'bout to pop," I said, while putting lotion on my face and hands.

I stared into the mirror and couldn't help but admire my reflection. At 250 pounds, I was bald with a full Rick Ross beard. I didn't look shit like I did back in 2003. My dark skin had a glow to it and my tattoos were really going to have the hos chasing a nigga. As I looked back at my celly, I couldn't help but laugh because he did the same shit every morning. He jumped right up to go email his bitch Treasure, his so called Wifey. Like clockwork, as soon as the doors popped open he was gone to the Corrlinks. Federal prisons have an email system called Corrlinks, and with the increase in technology the feds won't be left behind. Don't get it twisted, they be on that motherfucker watching everything you say.

I looked out my cell window and spotted my celly smiling as if he was in the screen. It was just the time I needed to bust a nut really quick. I put the towel up over the door and pulled out my stash of flicks of my mistress Bianca. I've got a wifey, but Bianca was sick with it. She was a redbone, kept her toes done, had a fat ass, nice titties, and long hair. She was like a light version of Nia Long. The one picture I chose to slaughter had her best friend Treasure in it. That's crazy isn't it? The skin flick I have of my bitch has my celly's wifey in it. I can't front, she was a bad bitch too.

After getting a few strokes in, the buzzer for chow time went off. It was time to eat that bullshit ass food. As I stepped in the chow hall, I couldn't help but notice how many niggas wanted to speak to me now that I was as short as a Chinese man's wiener. It was all good though, I was leaving my nigga with all of my shit anyway. A lot of those niggas were bustas for real. That was one thing I learned in prison, niggas act just like bitches and always have their hands out looking for something from a nigga.

I smashed to the homies table where all the Cali Bloods sat. This pissed my Up North homies off because I fucked with the West Coast niggas more than my own. But if you're real, you're real. Fuck where you're from. As I sat down and took in the scenery around me, I saw all the separation and all the racial barriers. I couldn't help but be happy that in just a few days I was going to be leaving this dump. Jail was no place for a nigga such as me, but you live and you learn.

After smashing out the chow hall, I made my way back to the tier to get dressed to go workout. I was so fucking burnt out. I was three days short and still on some bullshit carrying Bethlehem. I called my knife Bethlehem because when she hits your ass, you were going to be calling God to help you. I was too short, but shit could go up at any minute.

Bzzzzz!

The slave bell went off. I took my ass outside to do pull-ups and pushups. I fucking hated this midwest heat. Summertime in

3

Kansas felt more like Alabama. I could have sworn I saw the devil himself doing burpies.

"Yo, Chance!" I heard somebody call out.

Looking in the direction the call was coming from, I could see it was my nigga, L.J. He was short too.

"What's good, my nigga?" he asked.

"Sucka duckin' and staying out the way. What's good?" I asked, trying to get back to what I was about to do.

As usual he wasn't talking about shit so I got back to working out.

TWO HOURS LATER...

I had a good workout. Then it was time to hit that shower because the yard in Leavenworth smelled like cats. I decided to call wifey first. Dialing my wifey Lanise's number, I awaited to hear her voice.

"Hey, sexy," she would always say before the operator came on.

"You have a prepaid blah, blah, blah," the operator finished. Now I could talk to my baby.

"Hey bae, guess what?" she asked, sounding all excited.

"What's good, boo?" I asked her.

"Well, I know my man wanna ride in style so I'm about to go pick up a lil' sum 'in' for you to come home too," she said, sounding very proud of herself.

"What you got me, baby?" I asked her eagerly.

"Well, I got you the Infinity truck you always talk about," she started to explain. "A 2011 QX56, black-on-black with some nice 28's. I picked it out myself, bae. I bought it cash."

She went on the whole fifteen minutes until the call ended.

Satisfied with our talk, I got my black ass in the shower. I couldn't help but to think about the streets and how another strike would bust my ass. My co-defendant and I hit three banks before they caught us. When I was on the run, I hid $300 thousand dollars in my father's crib. In a few more days, I would be able to get my hands on that money. I could picture myself spending like there was no tomorrow. They only sentenced me for robbing one bank. They couldn't prove that I did the other two and they didn't have a weapon. They only gave us the minimum: ten years.

Lanise had enough money to hold her down since I've been gone, but I didn't let her know how much I really had or where I put my shit. Fucking around with her, I'd be broke. My mistress, Bianca, had a nigga open and I couldn't wait to bust that ass when I touched down.

Hopping out the shower, I made my way back to the cell and ran into Nu'voe.

"What's poppin'?" I asked as I watched him skillfully twisting a joint.

He had been a little distant knowing that I was about to roll out but I understood.

"You want some of this?" he asked me, while pulling on the joint.

"That's green or K2?" I asked.

"It's K2, homie," he busted out laughing before passing me the joint. "You know I wouldn't do you like that. I need you on dem streets nigga," he stated with concern.

I can't front, after about six pulls, I was high as shit. I don't know what they put in that shit, but it was some crucial.

"Ayo, I gotta holla at my lil' bitch in medical before I roll. You already know I'm gonna pass her off," I told Nu'voe as I lotion up and put a dab of Usher oil on.

I was high as shit as I made my way to medical to holler at my big girl, Ms. Burnes. Now Ms. Burnes was a white girl from Topeka, Kansas. She weighed about 280 pounds and trained to go. This big bitch could suck sand out of cement. She stayed dropping that sack, but today I needed her to get on some gangster shit. She smiled when I entered her office.

"You know I'm gonna be lonely when you leave me right?" she moaned as I sucked her titties.

I had to hold one tittie with both hands. Those motherfuckers were huge. I got her nice and warm before I popped the question.

"I need you, baby," I tried to sound as convincing as possible.

"What-what you- you need, just sa-say it, baby," she moaned as she responded.

I stopped sucking her titties and pulled out Uncle Elroy. This should seal the deal right here, I thought before I spoke.

"Look I need a cell phone by tomorrow. It's for my celly"

She continued to jerk me off, licking her fat, chapped ass lips as she smiled at me. I tried my hardest to hold my food down, but pussy in jail is the best pussy. I fucked that fat bitch like she was Halle Berry.

"I think I can make that happen. What's he gonna do for me?" she flirted.

"The same thing I'm doing now," I said, hoping she would mention it before I did.

"You know what I need, right?" she asked as she rolled over and pulled down her scrub pants.

NO TRUSTPASSING

This was some bullshit. I was about to go home and was forced to fuck a whale. Fuck it, I thought to myself. I gotta make sure my homie's straight.

****

I was strolling back to my unit when I noticed my celly's name on the list for legal mail.

"I wonder what that's about," I mumbled to myself as I approached my cell.

Nu'voe was nowhere in sight so I played the room and gathered my thoughts. Bianca was on my mind real heavy. I was really feeling her, and I know she was feeling me too. Every time I called, she always had some good shit to say to a nigga and I liked that. I had to move smoothly, and I had to stay away from that bitch, Treasure. She had been talking real slick on the phone. I knew I could hit that, but I wouldn't cross my nigga Nu'voe like that. Loyalty is Royalty!

Damn, that pedicure felt good to a bitch's feet. I had been walking around and working in heels all week and finally had a chance to kick back and relax. I was so tense and even more stressed. My man went to jail and left me to fend for myself. Don't get me wrong, I had a little paper but it was not like when my baby was home. It just felt like history was repeating itself.

As far back as I can remember my father used to be a pimp. I was only seven but there are some things that a child could never forget. I spent so many nights home alone eating canned foods and Ramen noodle soups. Then there were the nights when my parents were home. I've witnessed my mom getting the shit kicked out of her by my drunken father. Even though he used to physically abuse my mom, he somehow managed to provide for his one and only daughter. At seven years old, I felt like a true princess. Like a thief in the night, my royalties were snatched from me.

It was a hot summer day when I came home from school eager to show my dad the purple star I received in class. As soon as I stepped foot in my door I knew something was wrong. The house was empty. It wasn't until sundown that my mother came home. I ran to her and jumped in her arms, waiting to see daddy coming in behind her but she was alone.

I asked her, "Where is daddy?"

The look on her face was so cold and stern. She squatted to be eye-level with me and removed her big sunglasses from her face. That's when I noticed that she had a black eye.

"What's wrong, mommy?" I asked unable to hold back my tears.

She never answered my questions. She simply told me to pack my stuff.

All I could remember is grabbing my blanky and the Koala bear my daddy bought for me on my seventh birthday. We rushed out of the apartment and I never saw my father again. When I finally became a teenager at the age of thirteen the void of not having my father caused me to rebel against my mother. Since that day when she rushed me out of my castle, I've seen countless men come in and out of my mama's room. I waited and waited, hoping my dad would come back for me but it never happened! The one thing that did happen was the growing hatred for my mother. One day, shit hit the fan. We came to blows and she sent me to my grandmother's house for good.

Look at me now. I have long hair, high-yellow red skin complexion, and a body out of this world. I'm Treasure Dominique Simmons, the bastard daughter of a pimp, raised by his bottom bitch, my mother. I'm not mad at it though. I stay draped in the latest designer wear so you know them chicks in high school hated on me. Friends came a dime a dozen, and somehow I was either crossed or hated by my own.

Some called me stuck up, others called me conceited, but to me I'm just Treasure; my daddy's little Princess. Trust is something I knew nothing about. Every man I encountered hurt me deeply. From my father to my first love Maurice, who cheated on me with my best friend at the time. Fuck that trust and love shit. Niggas ain't shit.

"Treasure! Treasure!" someone called out, breaking my train of thought.

I looked over and it was my girl Bianca.

"What in the hell are you over there thinking about? You was gone girl," she said, while laughing.

I looked over at her then twisted up my face.

"What do you want heffa? I'm doing somethin' you haven't done in a long time. Thinking!" I said as I tried to get comfortable while listening to Diamond instigate in the background.

"She told ya ass didn't she, B?" she teased.

We all busted out laughing. Through all the bullshit I went through years ago, I finally found two chicks that I could call my friends, and they were right here by my side. Bianca was a hand full. She'd never worked a day in her life. Her daddy spoiled the shit out of her, and I envied that because that's what my dad was supposed to be doing for me. She stood 5'9" without heels on. She wore flawless, almond brown skin with big titties and an ass to die for. When she entered a room, she demanded attention. Sexiness burst from her pours. She was the high maintenance type so if a nigga wasn't paid he didn't stand a chance.

Diamond was my BFF. As black as she was, you would think she chose the wrong name, but when you looked at her neck and wrist you would understand. The six carat diamond pendant she wore could light up a dark room. Now, I know a lot of dark skinned girls, and I know the stigma they carry, but she was by far the baddest dark skinned bitch I had ever met. She had long, straight hair, and she and Bianca usually fought over whose hair was the longest. She had a circular pie shaped face and a cute set of dimples. She wasn't blessed with tits like me and Bianca, but with that ass she could turn heads at a blind man's convention. We had a lot of ups and downs between us, but those were my girls.

I've been friends with Diamond for a long time. She was the first girl I met when I moved in with my grandmother. She was the one that introduced me to Bianca a few years back, and we have been tight ever since. When she graduated college with an Associate's degree in Accounting I had no choice but to hire her to help me keep the books straight at the shop. *Face 2 Face* was my salon and we offered exclusive bath and body treatments. I had a manicurist, pedicurist, massage therapist, and bio-facialist. It was pretty laid out, and located in downtown San Diego right next to Horton Plaza Mall. It was 1,550 square feet with marble floors and high ceilings. My man Nu'voe left it to me right before the feds kidnapped him four years ago.

"So Treasure, what we doing tonight?" Diamond asked.

She was always ready to go clubbing. I didn't look at her when I answered.

"I don't know. It doesn't matter to me," I said with my eyes closed.

Bianca commented as well. "Please, let's not go to one of those low budget, broke ass nigga spots this weekend," she said, while staring at her nails.

Diamond and I both looked at her conceited ass and smiled. She dropped her Chanel shades over her eyes and ignored us both.

I got myself back to a comfortable position and thought about my man. I met Nu'voe one night in Club XO. It was something about his approach, his swagger, and his demeanor that separated him from the rest. We exchanged numbers and to my surprise he called the next morning and took me to breakfast. Long story short, he swept me off of my feet with his humor and the way he protected me. In a lot of ways, I could see my dad in him. Next thing you know, I was head over hills for this man and doing all my wife duties.

Damn, I'm weak for him and the more I think about it I get mad at myself for allowing it to happen. When the FBI took him away from me I was left all alone again. Wishful thinking came back and bit me in my ass. Here I am abandoned and mad at the world. Deja Vu.

CHAPTER THREE
NU'VOE

It was six o'clock in the morning and this big head nigga was up like it was one o'clock in the afternoon. He had been making noise since four or five this morning. If it was up to his ass, I wouldn't get any sleep. He was going home in a day and so sleep had been hard to come by for him. Chance's hard acting ass wasn't going to tell anybody, but I know the real, his ass was scared to death!

I couldn't blame him though. He had spent eight and half years behind this 100 year old Leavenworth Penitentiary wall, but it still didn't give him the right to keep me up. A player like myself needs his beauty sleep. That's why I'm pushing forty, but look like I'm twenty-five. One thing about being behind these walls is that it preserves you and gives you plenty of time to think. Today is one of those thinking days for me.

Looking at my celly, the memory of how we met crossed my mind. It was the summertime of '08 and the tension on the yard was heavy between the Hispanics and the Blacks. A riot broke out and I found myself back-to-back with a big bear-looking nigga fighting for our lives. Two cats from two different parts of the world came together and saved each other's lives. We put in some work and had each other's back through the bullshit.

Ever since then, Chance and I had been joined at the hip. If you saw one of us, you saw both of us, whether it was breakfast, lunch, dinner, yard, or movies. Rumor on the yard was that if you fucked with one of us, you might as well fuck with the other one because we were surely coming.

My thoughts jumped from my celly to my boo thang Treasure. Damn, she always seemed to find her way into my thought process. It's probably because she was still a major factor in my life. She was co-owner to almost everything I owned. Her name was present on all my paperwork from dental bills to death wills. What was really fucking with me is the fact that her pussy was the last pussy I had. Sometimes when I close my eyes and think about her, I swear to God I can smell her. Her breath, her Burberry perfume, her pussy! I know it sounds crazy, but it's the truth. It's something about doing time that enhances the male senses.

The day the feds showed up at my door changed my life forever. I went from a man pushing seven figures to a nigga trying to figure out my next move. I went from Benzes and shopping sprees in Acapulco to tennis shoes and commissary shopping. Imagine that! Five years later and I'm still effected by it. In just fourteen more months this living nightmare would be over. I was indicted on a conspiracy to distribute fifteen hundred pounds of weed over the phone. Already being a convicted felon, I pleaded out and received 96 months in federal custody.

I got up to see if I had any emails. I was hoping that my baby would have hollered at me by then.

"No emails." The system had to be tripping. I should have had some emails. "Aye, Double-O! I hollered at the homie that was sitting next to me at the computer.

"What's up, Nu'voe? He asked".

"You got some hits on this mother fucker?" I asked.

"Yeah, I got five homeboy," he replied with a smirk on his face. "Even though a nigga locked up these breezies be at me. Feel me? How many you got he asked me?

"I ain't got a damn thang, 'O. I'mma holla atcha later."

"Alright, homeboy."

A little disappointed that I didn't have any emails, I headed back to my cell. When I reached the door, I noticed the window was blocked and a towel was up covering the slot. There was one or two things that could be going on: Either Chance was in there dropping the kids off or he was drowning his future babies. Knowing him, he was making love to Palmetta the hand. It's a damn shame this nigga was going home in less than seventy-two hours, and he was still jacking off. Ten minutes later, he was done and I was in there doing the same thang!

LATER THAT DAY...

I had just finished squeezing on a stick of weed when I heard my name being called over the loudspeaker.

"Inmate Davoe 03755-298, please report to the counselor's office."

What the fuck! Somebody dropped a dime on me was my first thought because I was high as a kite.

I hurried up and freshened up. Visine for the eyes, a little cologne to cover up the smell, and about two quarts of warm water just in case they tried to pull the whoopy wham on me and piss test a nigga gotsta be more careful. They say this new shit going around here called K2 doesn't show up in your system but with only a calendar year left I couldn't take any chances.

Now that everything was taken care of, I pushed to the counselor's office. Upon my arrival, I noticed that there was a line with about six or seven inmates waiting to see the counselor. I spotted my Esé partner Lil' Scrappy in line.

"What's this shit about?" I asked him.

"Some legal mail shit, homes." Lil' Scrappy answered with his strong Mexican accent. "They fuckin' wit' my money right now Nu'voe, feel me homie?"

Lil' Scrappy was the ticket man, and he was trying to get back to booking tickets. In the 20 minutes that he was waiting to see the counselor, Lil' Scrappy had missed out on at least 50 to 60 dollars.

Hearing that it was only about legal mail made my mind relax, and I stood there chopping it up with Lil' Scrappy about which teams were going to cover the spreads in football that week. Then it was my turn to see the counselor, Ms. Johansen. She was bad and she knew it. She was an Italian woman with clear skin and a nice shape in her mid-40's. The thing that made her bad was the fact that she had a good job, her credit was A-1, and her attitude toward inmates and convicts was one of understanding and respect.

On any given day, you could find a line of thirsty ass niggas outside of her office. Niggas didn't even want nor need anything. They just wanted to be in her presence.

"Mr. Nu'vaar Davoe, how are you today?" Ms. Johansen asked me.

"A lot better now that I'm talking to you. I hope this legal mail you got for me will put some mo' sunshine in my life," I flirtatiously responded as I brandished a wide smile.

After fifteen years of dealing with all type of niggas, Ms. Johansen was used to the flirting game and brushed me off as she said, "Mr. Davoe, you have legal mail so I need you to sign here confirming that you received it and that we opened it up in your presence."

"I aint signing my life over to you am I?" I asked still attempting to flirt.

After shooting my shot down, I realized she wasn't going for it. I grabbed my legal mail and pushed back towards my cell. On the way I stopped by the computers to see if they were still tripping. When I logged on, in blue letters it read: *YOU HAVE 3 NEW MESSAGES.*

About time, I thought. I clicked on the first envelope. It was a message from Treasure that read: WHEN YOU GET THE CHANCE, HURRY UP AND CALL. THERE'S SOMETHING I NEED TO TELL YOU.

The next message was from my nephew that read:

UNK, THIS IS NEPHEW. I WAS JUST CHECKIN' ON U, HOLLA BACK.

The third envelope I clicked on was also from Treasure that read: NEVER MIND THAT FIRST MESSAGE BABY. I DON'T WANT TO WORRY YOU ABOUT MY PROBLEMS. YOU ALREADY HAVE ENOUGH ON YOUR PLATE. LOVE YOU 'TIL I'M GONE.

After I read the messages, I logged off the computer and doubled back to the phone to call Treasure. Obviously, something was bothering my baby and I wanted to know what. Three unsuccessful tries later, I gave up and slid to my cell.

9:35 P.M...

"Ten minutes to lockdown! Ten minutes to lockdown!" the C.O. yelled over the loudspeaker.

Damn, today went by fast, and I didn't even get to talk to my baby all day. Lately this had been a reoccurring thing. It seemed like the closer I got to coming home, the bumpier our relationship got. I chalked up not talking to her and exchanged a couple of when I get out stories with Chance's crazy ass then called it a night.

Getting up and starting my day at 5:30 in the morning, sleep quickly engulfed me thanks to my celly.

It seemed as soon as I was asleep, I was startled awake. I must have been dreaming or having a nightmare because I was soaked in sweat. I hopped off the top bunk and grabbed my watch to check the time.

"Damn, 2:27 a.m.!"

I put the watch back on the desk and was about to attempt to recapture my sleep when I noticed my legal mail I had received earlier. Between all the madness that was going on in here, being off balance by my baby's confusing messages, and that K2, reading my legal mail had slipped my mind. I grabbed the envelope, opened it up, and what it contained inside caused my heart to skip a beat and flutter all at the same time.

"What?" was the only word I could utter?

My breathing had become short and labored and my legs were weak and wobbly. I sat down in my government issued chair and re-read the letter: **UNITED STATES OF AMERICA VS. NU'VAAR DAVOE.**

I was being superseded indicted for money laundering, tax evasion, fraudulent information on property applications, and interstate commerce. The government was charging me with racketeering. With only fourteen months to the house, this was a living nightmare. If that wasn't enough, as I kept reading the indictment I read Treasure's name. My baby was also being indicted.

"Chance! Chance!" I yelled my celly's name, waking him up.

He jumped up so fast and reached for his five-inch jail-made knife.

"What crackin', huh? What's crackin'?" yelled my celly as he held the knife with a death grip and attempted to stand up.

He surprised the hell out of me. I never knew his big ass could move like that.

"Calm down nigga, wit'cha paranoid ass! It's me, fool," I said, praying that he didn't mistake me for somebody trying to get the drop on him.

At 250 pounds with a bone crusher in his hand and confined to this eight-by-twelve cell, this nigga would be hell to deal with.

"You scared the shit out of me, yo! What time is it anyway?" he asked with that Jersey accent along with an attitude.

I didn't answer him. I was too fucked up in the mind at the moment to say anything. I just threw the papers on his bed. Chance picked the indictment up and silently read it. No words came from him either even though it wasn't him being indicted. He still felt fucked up because his road dog was now in a sticky situation.

Finally, he spoke, "Get atcha lawyer, 'Vo. This shit here is major."

As if I didn't know that! From that point on all I could think about was my life!

CHAPTER FOUR
CHANCE

FIVE DAYS LATER...

Beep! Beep! Beep!
The sound of my wife's annoying ass alarm clock woke me from my deep sleep. You know when a nigga comes home, good sleep is well needed. Especially after all the years I had been gone. When I opened my eyes and looked over, I noticed my Shorty wasn't in the bed next to me. Suddenly, the smell of breakfast filled my nostrils. I sat up for a second only to lay back down for a good stretch. Bottom line, I had been home for five days and hadn't gotten shit done. Wifey had been fucking and sucking a nigga dry. She had been cooking five-star meals, getting a nigga all chunky, and fucking up my six-pack.

I hadn't been to my mother's gravesite, and I hadn't been to check on my father yet. I'm slipping.

My thoughts were interrupted by another one of Lanise's tricks. There she stood, holding a plate of food, wearing nothing but a garter belt, six-inch red bottom heels and her titties were fully exposed. She knows I love her titties. *Here we go*, I thought.

Slowly she began to feed me scrambled eggs, toast, turkey bacon, and grapes with a glass of freshly squeezed orange juice. When I dug into my food she began to feed herself, sucking me whole while I tried to eat.

"Fuck this shit," I mumbled, putting half the plate of food to the side on the dresser and y'all know what happened next.

Quickly I shitted, showered, and shaved. I dressed myself in a pair of True Religion denim jeans, a fitted, crispy white V-neck T-shirt, and a pair of solid black Prada sneakers. I made my way out the door. Hopping in my QX56, I made sure my first day home I got this motherfucker five percent tinted all the way around. That's how we rode around in Jersey. If it wasn't tinted, I wasn't in it. Before I pulled off, I fiddled with this dumb ass IPod until it came on to my Tupac selection. I fired up a blunt of Sour Diesel and rode out.

My P.O. was really sweet.

He just told me straight up, "No new cases!"

He made me promise to call once a month. That's all I needed to hear. I turned the AC on before rolling back the sunroof halfway so my stash box could open. The radio deck opened and voilà, a subcompact Glock 9, a cell phone, and ten Gs was there. That's for hotels, bail, or whatever.

I made my way to a local flower shop and picked up some roses to lay on my mom's gravesite in order to pay my respects. After an hour, I decided it was time to go see my pops. I figured I'd surprise him instead of calling.

Damn, I can't wait to get my money. I've got some real live shit to do, I thought to myself.

I called Bianca from my other phone. You know I can't have anybody calling while I'm with the wifey.

She answered on the third ring, sounding sexier than ever, "Hello."

"Hey sexy, it's me, Chance," I said into the receiver in case she didn't recognize the number.

"I know my baby's voice. What's up, and when you coming to see me?" she asked, sounding eager to see me in person.

"I'll be there in two weeks, tops." I told her. "I gotta make some moves so I can put you up in a better spot—"

She cut me off, and said, "Ooh daddy, I seen this nice ass condo close to where Treasure stays at,"

She whined like the spoiled brat she was.

"How much?" I asked her, curious to know the price.

She shot right back, "It's only two gran' a month if you renting, but I can get a good deal if we tryna buy it."

Knowing I couldn't tell her no, I agreed to come see the place when I got there.

As I pulled into my father's complex, I was about to disconnect the call until I asked, "How is Treasure?"

There was an awkward silence before she spoke again.

"Umm, she's good. Just stressing that's all. The damn feds keep fucking wit' her. Going to her house and they even came by the salon a few times. They all over her."

"Damn," was all I could say before we disconnected the call.

I'll call her later, but now I had some business to tend too. As I hopped out my truck I noticed that shit looked a little different around here. I didn't see my Pop's Cadillac when I pulled up but I figured he'd gotten something else to push since I'd been away. I walked up the steps and rang the doorbell. I heard the lock on the door unlatch.

The door opened just enough for me to peek in, and then a white woman in her 40s appeared at the door. My first thought was that my father must have gotten a caretaker to help out around the house. Then I looked at her again and our facial expressions where the same.

"Hello ma'am, I'm looking for my brother," I lied, not wanting to say my father.

Shaking her head from side-to-side she began to speak.

"Sorry, he doesn't live here," she replied, while trying to close the door on me.

I put my foot in the wedge to stop it.

"Wait, wait, wait," I pleaded. "Who lives in this house, ma'am?"

"It's just me and my Allen. If you don't leave I'll be forced to call the cops."

"Hold on, wait a minute. I didn't come to harm you, ma'am. I'm just looking for my brother that's all," I began to raise my voice.

"I've been living here for over four years, and before me it was some blacks. That's all I have to say," she said before slamming the door in my face.

I stood there stuck in shock. What the fuck does she mean that she's been living here over four years? Where's my dad, or better yet where's my fucking money? I had $300 thousand dollars buried in the attic, and she's telling me he doesn't live here. Shit, I'm going to get my money. I sat and contemplated. My pops is paralyzed. There's no way he could have found it. I have to get in there, and I have to get in there now."

Thinking fast on my feet, I called my homie Justin and had him meet me back in Jersey City in the Curry Woods projects. For safety reasons, none of my niggas knew where I laid my head. Seeing him pull up, I hopped out my truck and jumped in the Lexus GS300 with him. The clock read 2:36 p.m.

"Where too, homie?" he asked before pulling off.

"Go to the hoopty lot downtown," I directed him.

Moments later and some fast talking I left the lot with a Navy Blue 1987 Cutlass Supreme with dealer plates. I told Justin I'd call him later with the details, but right now my mind was on one thing and one thing only. My money!

I tried calling my father's cell phone but got the voicemail. I called my whole damn family tree and nobody had heard from him in months. It was like he disappeared off the face of the earth. I drove the Cutlass to my house and contemplated how I was gonna go about this. As much as I didn't want to, tonight I was running up in that house and laying something down for my money.

****

It was 9:17 p.m. when I parked on the outskirts of the housing complex. Now, anybody that knows about New Jersey, my pops lived in Belleville and that's an area where you get pulled over for, (D.W.B.) Driving While Black. So, I had to be extra careful about pulling this off. From where I was parked I could see the apartment and the exits. It was crazy because I had only been home five funky ass days, and I'm already throwing rocks at the pen. Fuck it because 300 G's was just that, 300 G's.

I bought a mini axe from the hardware store that fit snug in my North Face book bag. Checking the clip in my Glock 9, I slid on my leather Nike gloves. I wore an all-black North Face sweat suit with a ski-mask rolled up on my baldhead. I couldn't leave the house without my six-inch Kobar army issued knife. Jail has really got me on this knife shit. I said a quick prayer and headed out.

Crossing through some bushes and a small fence, I made my way to the back of the house. I knew this house like the back of my hand. I crept to the back porch and peeked through the kitchen window. The sport-coat draped over the chair let me know that Allen was in the building. I reached in my back pocket to retrieve my knife when a big ass light shinned on me.

"Oh shit!"

I tried my best to duck for cover then the unthinkable happened.

Boc! Boc! Boc!

Three shots rang out over my head then shattered glass fell on my body. I jumped to my feet quick and got the fuck out of there.

I know I'm in good shape but damn, I took one step over the fence and then next thing you know I was in my car. Being trained in the field of doing dirt I left my key in the ignition and the car running. I pulled off and headed home, but this shit was far from over.

"Where the fuck is my father?"

When I stepped foot in the house the look on my Shorty's face was a grimace. She looked like the devil himself. She sucked her teeth and stood to walk away from the couch.

"Ya ass going back to jail, and when you do I'm gone this time!" she said before disappearing up the stairs.

I entered the kitchen and caught a glimpse of myself in our full length mirror, and I could see why she was beefing with me. Here I stood in all black and due to me rushing I forgot to take the face mask off my head and the gloves off my damn hands. I was slipping and to make matters worse, I didn't have this on when I left the house earlier.

THE NEXT DAY...

I got up at eleven this morning and called my lil' homie, Justin. He was a loyal youngin' who I gave the game to before I caught my bid. He held shit down for me while I was gone; flicks, money on the books, all of that. You don't find them like that anymore. I sat where I slept last night, on the sofa, smoking a blunt and watching the Spanish news. That broad Chique is a beast. I did nine years watching her and the other chick Jackie. Wifey made her way to work without saying a word to me before she left. Shit, it was cool with me. I had 300 grand to get. I couldn't give a fuck about a bitch attitude.

Justin called my cell phone telling me he was at a nearby gas station so I quickly got dressed to go meet him. When I pulled up, he hopped in the truck with me. We rode around smoking a blunt and watching, Shotta's, on my TV screens. I decided to ride pass the house and scope it out for a second.

"What are we doing here?" Justin asked.

I was so high off the sour I told him the whole story from the beginning to the end. Under normal circumstances, I would have never done some foolish shit like that but it was my little man so I wasn't tripping.

Pulling on the blunt he asked me, "How you gonna get in there?" He took another drag. "Maybe you could act like the pizza man or somethin'."

When he said that, it sparked something in my head. Quickly I put my truck in drive and dropped him off. I made my way home to devise a plan to get my money, and then make good with my wifey. I cooked her some fried chicken, corn, and yellow rice. I prepared a hot bath for her then awaited her arrival.

By the time I was done feeding all three of her holes it was 10:30 p.m. I called a cab to take me to Jersey City and Lanise was so worn out that she never heard me leave. I paid my cabby twenty bucks to take me to My Florist Flower Shop located on Storms and Bergen Avenues. When we arrived there, the gate was closed which was cool with me.

"You going back to Newark, buddy?" the Arabic cab driver asked me.

"Nah, I'm cool. I'll take it from here," I said as I exited the cab.

I looked around and noticed all the company trucks with the My Florist logo alongside the vehicles.

"Cool," I mumbled as I pulled out the pulley from my sleeve and approached the Dodge Caravan with the logo plastered on the sides.

Now, you all know I'm a true Jersey nigga. A minute and a half flat, I was in, starting the ignition, and pulling away from the parking spot. I looked in the rear of the van and noticed a bouquet of roses that would come in handy. I headed back towards my home in Society Hill.

THE NEXT MORNING...

I let my Shorty take my truck and I pushed her Range Rover Sport just to be in something niggas hadn't seen me in and this too was five percent tinted all the way around. I parked in the Pep Boys parking lot, and then jogged over to the gas station where I parked the stolen van. In twenty minutes flat, I was standing in front of my dad's old apartment. I had to be smart on this one so I changed my attire. I put on a white button up shirt, a black tie, some slacks, and some black low-top Air Force Ones. I wore a fitted hat with my face mask under it with the bouquet of flowers in my left hand leaving my right to grab my weapon.

I read the mail box, DOYLE. *What the fuck kinda last name is that?* I thought to myself, while my heart was beating out of my chest. Ok, Chance let's do this. They call you Chance 'because you take Chances. I pumped myself up as I rang the doorbell. I let the flowers block the peephole in case she or he peeked out.

"Who is it?" a female's voice called out through the other side of the door.

"Delivery from a secret admirer, flowers for a Mrs. Doyle."

I had to think quickly. When I heard the locks unlatch and the door swung wide open I went into straight beast-mode.

I heard her say, "Aww, someone sent me some flowers—"

I pushed the shit out of her back into the house in one swift movement, stepping in and closing the door behind me.

She hit the floor and screamed, "Please don't hurt me!"

Quickly, I dropped my mask and pulled my weapon.

"Shut the fuck up and don't move. Who else is in here?" I asked while looking around.

"Nobody! I'm alone," she pleaded and began to cry. "Please don't hurt me!" she cried out, looking for some remorse.

She started shaking. She had to be about 45.

I kneeled down, pressing my gun against her temple.

"Look, this won't take long. Get up and let's head upstairs," I said as I helped her to her feet, still holding my gun to her.

As we passed by each room I investigated to the T, just in case Allen decided to bust a few more shots. Plus, I knew there was a gun in there somewhere. Satisfied with my room search, I tied her up with some bed sheets to restrain her. When I was done, both her hands and feet were tied to the bedpost and I gagged her mouth as well. I made my way to the attic, pulled my axe out from my pants leg, and went to work. Once I located the discolored floorboard, it was simple. After 30 minutes, I dug up the exact spot where my money was but there was a big problem, the bag was gone! I knew it was the spot because the manila envelope containing phone numbers to my old connects was still there so whoever took the money felt this wasn't important.

"Fuck, Fuck, Fuck!" I shouted. "My father got my money," I said to myself.

I was pissed! So pissed that I contemplated blowing Mrs. Doyle's brains out on G.P. but decided not to. It wasn't her fault. I picked myself up and headed to where Mrs. Doyle was tied up at. Dropping my axe to the floor and a look of panic consumed her face as she turned beet red. She began to cry and mumble something through her gag.

"I'm not gonna hurt you, lady. I'm gonna untie one arm and you can do the rest, ok?" I assured her.

I removed her gag, and she thanked me for not harming her. I made my way to the exit.

I dumped the van and got back to Lanise's truck to make my way home. This shit was crazy. How did I get played out of my hard earned money?

"I'm fuckin' broke! Broke, broke, broke!" I yelled as I banged on the steering wheel. "What the fuck am I going to do now?" I asked myself as I looked in the rearview mirror.

I felt sorry for the man looking back at me.

Before I knew it I was home in my bed with a banging ass headache and a bad attitude. I made the decision to kill my father whenever I caught up with him; no ifs, ands, or butts about it. I lie on the soft pillow and passed out.

****

When I came to it was dark out.

"Damn, I was out cold."

I sat up and called my lil' homie Justin so that he could take me to get my Cutlass in the morning. A female's voice answered.

"Hello," she answered with an annoyed tone.

"May I speak to Justin, please?" I asked as kindly as possible.

"Umm, you could talk to him if you bail him out!" she shot back with much attitude.

What she said caught me off guard.

"What you just say?"

"You heard me, nigga! Bail!" she reiterated. "He done got his dumbass locked up in Belleville tryna rob some white folks."

When I heard Belleville and white folks my stomach did a back flip. That was Mrs. Doyle. *Grimmey ass nigga!* I thought to myself.

"Ok ma'am, thank you," I hung up before she could say anything else. I sat there in deep thought. "Damn, my lil' soldier crossed me like that? If he makes bail, I'll put so many fire balls in his head they gonna have to cremate his ass. And just to think, I was gonna bring this nigga to my crib."

I had to get my shit together. I had been home a week and all the positive shit I was telling the fellas was pure BULLSHIT out the window. I'm right back at it, but this time it's for a good reason. I'm fucking broke! I looked at the manila envelope, knowing I could call Cochise and get ten keys brought to my doorstep in two days. All them Paisa's I plugged in with down in Mexico were waiting on my call. That's the worst thing they could have done was put me in the feds with real niggas from all over the world. I'm plugged in Cali, St. Louis, Nebraska, Kansas City, wherever. I still had a little something left, and Lanise did well with the money I left her by opening the dump truck business. Shit wasn't looking good for the kid, but I'm a rider for real so it is what it is. I knew what I needed to do. I had to have a family gathering that would bring that nigga out of hiding. *Yeah, that's it and I'll put my bitch on Facebook to find his ass*, I thought to myself. It was on and popping. Lord knows I didn't wanna stamp my dad.

CHAPTER FIVE
NU'VOE

Sitting in my cell, I realized it had been five days since Chance took his ass home. That was a real good look for him. He deserved it even though I had a strong feeling the knucklehead nigga might not be ready for the streets yet. All he did, day and night, was talk about how he was going to do this and do that. Not once did he talk about doing the right thing. After doing eight and a half years you would think that he would have gotten the picture. However, who really is ready for the streets? I wasn't even sure if I was ready, either.

I missed my nigga. When he was here, I had a true ear to talk to. For those past five days, I had been in deep conversations with the walls. True enough, I'd come to find out that those walls were the best listeners. They didn't talk back, argue, and most importantly I could tell them any and everything and not once have they repeated a word to anybody. That's true loyalty if you ask me.

I had a visit scheduled with my lawyer about a bullshit ass indictment they slapped on me and my baby Treasure. I knew she had to have been wigging out. Baby ain't never did a day in jail in her life. One time she was pulled over and taken down to the substation for a D.U.I. and she called me every fifteen minutes for eight hours crying, screaming, and begging me to come get her. I would have, if I could have. If you've ever been arrested for a D.U.I., then you know that they keep you in custody until you sober up. So after those eight hours of sobering up, my baby was released on her own recognizance and I was then able to pick her up.

To this day I still tease her about that incident.

"Davoe - 249 you have a visit! Davoe - 249 you have a visit!" announced the C.O. over the loudspeaker in the unit.

Half the time you couldn't even hear or understand shit when they spoke through them cheap speakers over the loud ass niggas playing cards and dominoes. Knowing this the little Crip homie Murk from Harlem 30's out of Denver, Colorado rushed to my cell to let me know that I had a visit.

"Nu'voe!" he yelled.

"What's up, Murk?" I asked.

"Look at my boy. He's 'bout to be dancin' on that flo," he said. "You got a vizo, homie. They just called your name."

Getting visits way out here in Kansas, home to Dorothy and Tito, was a big thing.

"This ain't no visit from a bitch," I explained. "This my lawyer 'bout that bullshit I told you about."

We chopped it up about a whole bunch of nothing, while I got dressed in my starched and ironed khaki colored imitation dickie suit. Although I'm from the streets of San Diego, California, when I got home khaki color and dickie suits were the last thing I wanted to see or wear.

Fully dressed, I pushed to the visiting room. The entire five minutes it took me to get there my stomach did gymnastics. I was as nervous as a ho in church, and I didn't even know why. Something just didn't feel right. When I sat down across the table from my lawyer, the look on his face confirmed my gut feeling. Something was definitely not right. We shook hands. He began to explain the indictment to me, which I already knew and understood. Then he hit me with a bomb shell. My lawyer handed me the governments witness list. On that list were the names of twenty people. Fifteen of them I didn't know, two were business reps of mine that I vaguely remembered, and two were confidential informants. The name I couldn't help but recognize caused me to re-read.

It read: GOVERNMENT'S WITNESS. *This can't be right,* I thought.

"What's this shit!" I asked my lawyer, fearing the worse.

"I was hoping that you could tell me," he replied.

Reading the name over-and-over again, my stomach became tight. It felt like I had swallowed a half gallon of spoiled milk. I was instantly sick.

"Treasure, baby what you doin'?" I silently asked.

As soon as the question left my lips I already had the answer. It was clear as day. The feds had put the pressure on her until she broke. It probably didn't even take that long either, knowing Treasure.

This shit was all my fault. I shouldn't have involved her this deep. She was on everything connected to me. Everything!

"Mr. Davoe," my lawyer began, "this is what I've come up with. From the looks of things, the D.A. has you by the balls. Especially since the lady is willing to testify against you. If I were you, I would take the first plea that they offer."

"First offer!" I shot back.

"Well yes, Mr. Davoe. You're a convicted felon with priors and you're being charged with racketeering. If we go to trial and lose— Well, you're looking at life behind bars."

My lawyer raised his eyebrows and used that bullshit ass lawyer's voice.

"What you think the plea gonna look like?" I asked.

I really didn't want to go to trial, lose, and then spend the rest of my life behind bars. Fuck that. Right then and there I was ready to hear what these feds were talking about. Everybody knew these people had a ninety percent conviction rate when going to trial. I wasn't going to be a fool.

"I'm glad you asked," replied my lawyer as he dug into his briefcase and pulled out another stack of papers. "Here it is right here."

He had a dumbass smirk on his face. I swear I wanted to slap the shit out of him. He's already got me a plea bargain!

As I grabbed the papers and read the first few lines, the sickness in my stomach turned into anger. The D.A. was offering me 327 to 368 months in jail!

"What the fuck is this, and what you want me to do with it?" I asked, raising my voice.

My uproar was catching the attention of a few of the other visitors in the room.

"Mr. Davoe." my lawyer timidly said my name.

He was caught off guard by my response. How did he expect me to react to that shit? Anybody in their right mind wouldn't sign any shit like that. They were offering me up to 30 years. That was life behind bars. Yeah right! My dumbass lawyer was sitting there with that dumbass look on his face, trying to convince me to take it.

"Mr. Davoe, I know this is your life and this sentence might seem long but—."

"Might seem long?" I cut him off.

"You need to make a decision today," My lawyer said with his hands up, hoping to calm me down. "After today, this offer will be off the table and it only gets worse from here. Like I said at the beginning, they have you by the balls."

As my lawyer spoke, he was sweating profusely. I couldn't take it anymore. At that moment, something inside of me clicked and I lost all sense of normal thinking.

"You know what, Mr. Sarringossoff," I began. "I've been dealing with you for a long, long time and up until now I've respected you to the fullest. But fuck you, fuck that D.A., and fuck that plea bargain," As I spoke, spit flew out my mouth and landed on his forehead. "I want you off my case, not now but right now."

During me cursing his ass out, I managed to find myself on top of the man. The C.O.'s in the visiting room had to rush over to save him. Two more minutes and I probably would have caught another case. With him off of my case I would have to get me a public defender, also known as a public pretender. Shit, the way I was thinking was that my lawyer and the D.A. were working together. Instead of giving them my life, they were going to have to take it. Looking at all that time with a plea bargain, I was going to trial and the woman I loved was going to have to bury me alive.

I left the visiting room and headed outside to the yard to walk some laps around the track. I had to get my thoughts together. With each lap I walked, my future became blurrier. With each lap, my decisions became more difficult. I was going to have to do something that I knew I would regret. Back in my cell, I dug out the cell phone Chance had left me and dialed his number. When he answered I laid out what I was going through and explained my plan. I was hoping he was with it. Without hesitation, my nigga was all in. Probably more for himself than for me. Between me propositioning 50 G's and him already losing 300 hundred G's, the offer was too good to pass up.

Now this is where everything got tricky.

CHAPTER SIX
TREASURE

As I lay on my back with my feet pointed up towards the ceiling, the emotions running through me were crazy. For one, the FBI had been coming to my house and my place of business for the past six months. They had been threatening me, and saying I better help them if I wanted to help myself. At first, I really didn't know what they were talking about and at the time I really didn't care. Then one day during a visit to my home they showed me pictures of business transactions. They even let me hear some recorded messages and telephone conversations. They told me that I was a major player in a lot of illegal activities that had been going on. Even worse, I could possibly spend the rest of my life in jail! Now, that got a bitch's attention.

In jail for the rest of my life! There was no way I could ever do that. I went to jail one time for a D.U.I. and practically lost my mind. I couldn't even begin to imagine being in jail for the rest of my life. I would rather be dead, and that's honestly not something I wanted for myself either. So, when the police explained to me how I could help myself I agreed. They told me all I had to do was tell them how I obtained everything I owned. Of course everyone who knew me, knew how I had received my possessions.

Although I wasn't raised in the streets, I knew that the feds were asking me to snitch on Nu'voe I played with the decision for a while. I wasn't sure whether or not I should tell, but as time went on my attachment to Nu'voe weakened. I thought more about my freedom. I wanted my freedom more than anything.

To me, he started to resemble my father in such a negative way. Even though the police had taken him away, there was no getting around the fact that he had left me! It was just like when my father left me.

The police had plenty of tricks up their sleeves when it came to getting a witness to cooperate, and they used a few against me. From showing me pictures of Nu'voe out at different restaurants with different women to showing me that my signature was on everything that he owned. That was the icing on the cake. That's when it all clicked in my head. Although I wasn't walking the streets, Nu'voe was still doing to me what my father was doing to my mother.

He was pimping me!

Don't get me wrong, I loved my father. He was my king, but I despised what he did to my mother. To this day, I feel as though the way he treated my mother is the reason why our family is no longer together.

Now, if that wasn't enough, ever since the FBI came to my house, I've been off balance and haven't been thinking right.

"Uuuuunnnnhhhhh! Oh shit! Shit! Shit! My man is in jail and I've been weak, shit! Fuck me! Yes, fuck me!"

I know it was wrong, but I had been fucking Nu'voe's nineteen-year-old nephew, Lil' Face for the past couple of years. At first, he used to just come by the house to wash the cars, feed the dogs, and make sure that his uncle's woman was alright. Then one day he stopped by right when I had just gotten out of the shower. I was in the process of crying because I had just made the decision to tell on Nu'voe. He knocked on the door.

I answered and let him in.

Noticing that I was crying, he asked what was wrong with me. I couldn't tell him the truth so I made up a quick lie, and told him that one of my close family members had died. He gave me a tight hug and told me that everything was going to be alright. I knew I had convinced him.

At the time, all I had on was a terrycloth bathrobe with nothing underneath. Lil' Face knew that I was naked too because the robe wasn't tied tight and my goodies were peeking through. When we broke our embrace, Lil' Face's hormones were bulging. The imprint in his Akademiks sweatpants made that confirmation. Seeing this, my nipples instantly became hard. Shit, it had been four and a half years since I had some dick and I lost my cool. The weakness took control of me. I dropped my robe and attacked him like I was a predator in the jungle.

Lil' Face was only eighteen-years-old at the time, but he had the body of a grown man. He fucked like one too. That was why whenever I needed something fixed, I called Lil' Face, the young maintenance man.

I had been trying to work up enough courage to tell Nu'voe, but every time I got ready to do so my mouth and brain would not co-exist. My last attempt was through an e-mail, but I just couldn't bring myself to tell him in that way. I didn't think I would ever be able to tell him. It might have sounded crazy, but I loved Nu'voe with everything in me.

"Oh my God! I'm about to cum!"

Even while having bomb as sex with his nephew, I still managed to think of Nu'voe. It was our little secret. The only other person who knew about my secret was the man upstairs and my diary. Diamond was always telling me that I was playing with fire for the crazy decisions I've made, including helping the police. There were two things that her black ass refused to understand. She wasn't the bitch that went four and a half years without some dick, nor was the FBI knocking on her door threatening to put her bourgeois ass in jail for life.

Like I said, I still loved Nu'voe, but I was scared and lost. Shit, his ass shouldn't have left me in the first place. It's his entire fault!

Looking at Lil' Face he reminded me so much of Nu'voe in so many ways. He was handsome, tall, and well-groomed. He was very business minded to be so young. Not to mention, he fucked me just as good as Nu'voe.

Ring! Ring!

My phone rung and interrupted my after sex moment with Lil' Face. I had just cum and my legs were still shaking. I gathered myself to take a look at my phone then I sent the call to voicemail.

"Who was that?" Lil' Face asked as he gave me a serious look.

"That was your uncle," I answered as I hopped out the bed and slid on my DKNY boy shorts that read, I LOVE MY BOYFRIEND across the ass. Nu'voe had bought me them for my birthday. I immediately felt guilty and Lil' Face seemed to feel the same because he hopped up, got dressed, and headed to the door.

Before he walked out the door, he turned to me, and said, "Treasure, either you tell him or I will. That's my uncle, and I can't keep lying to him."

I looked him in his eyes and nodded my head. Little did he know the situation at hand was way deeper than sex. Sooner than later, Nu'voe's problems were going to be much bigger than just his girlfriend and nephew fucking!

CHAPTER SEVEN
CHANCE

It was 5:35 a.m. when I opened my eyes. Damn, I can't sleep for shit. I'm fuckin' stressing. I still couldn't believe that my pops ran off with my cash. To think I took good care of his bad feet having ass. Then to make matters worse my little nigga Justin showed the ultimate sign of betrayal. It was crazy. What? Do I have a sign on my forehead, I'm easy to cross? I wanted to stamp both of their asses.

****

My nigga, Nu'voe, reached out to me. The news he dropped on me was too much to handle. One side of me was thinking, Chance 50 G's is up for the grabbin' and you need this money, nigga. Then the other side of me was thinking, Chance, this ain't the average victim. This is this nigga's wifey, Treasure. Then I decided to go to Cali, smoke some good bud, fuck the shit out of Bianca, and then push Treasure's shit back so far that it would have her in the newspaper for weeks. Shit, Barack Obama could have gotten hit as much as I needed the money.

I had to figure out how I was going to tell Lanise that I was going to California for a few weeks. I knew she was going to flip, but I couldn't care about that. I made my nigga a promise and my word is all I've got.

I laid in bed lost in thought. Rolling over I noticed how good Lanise looks when she sleeps. I had been so caught up in my own shit that I hadn't even fucked her in the past few days. I know she knew something was up.

My baby was moving around a lot, waking up. I watched her as she walked her naked ass to the shower, putting an extra step on her walk. She knew I was watching. As the shower water came on and the steam escaped from under the door I figured what better time than now.

I approached the bathroom, listening to her hum the Mary J. Blige's song, *Be Without You*. I slid the shower curtain back and stepped in with her as she turned to face me. I grabbed her chin and brought her lips to meet mine. We kissed as if it were our last time. I heard moans escape her mouth as our bodies pressed against each other. I went from her lips, to her neck, and then down to her breast, cupping each one in my hand, taking my time and giving attention to each one. I stepped back and took in her beauty.

Lanise was a bad bitch at twenty-eight years old and weighing 130 pounds. Little mama stood five foot, five inches with hair that draped to the middle of her back. Her half Cuban features gave her skin a golden look. She truly belonged in a Straight Stuntin' Magazine with the measurements she was carrying around. Thirty-eight C-cups with the dark nipples, and a forty-two-inch ass that stood on its own. Trust me; I had to bust my gun plenty of times behind her sexy ass. That's my wifey.

I spun her around and knowing how daddy liked it she locked her legs and bent over slightly, reaching back leading me into her wetness.

Damn, my baby's shit was tight as I felt her walls wrap around John Shotty. I was so lost in the moment. Lost in lust. Before I knew it, I was releasing inside of her as she tightened her grip around me, making me weak in the knees. To top it off, she turned around, dropped to her knees, and cleaned me up right.

Getting every drop, she emptied me out. We washed off and hopped out of the shower.

Getting ready for work, I stood behind her and watched her do her make-up. The look on my face said it all.

"What's wrong, bae?" she asked me while putting her hair in a slick ponytail.

Dropping my head, I answered, "I'm broke, baby."

She looked at me through the mirror like I was playing. She turned to face me.

"What do you mean, baby?"

I explained to her about the stash at my pops house. I even told her how I ran up in that motherfucker and that was why she saw me dressed like that a few nights before. When I told her about me taking a trip to Cali she was reluctant at first, but she gave me all the support I needed and told me to hurry home.

Before I left, I checked to see if Justin had come home yet, but he hadn't. I checked in with my P.O. to make sure I was cool. Then I made my way to the bank and withdrew fifteen stacks for a little pocket money. I parked the Cutlass in the garage, busted two nuts in my bitch, and made my way to Newark Airport.

****

I landed at L.A.X. at 6:15 p.m. I was over dressed and stuck out like a sore thumb with Timberland boots on. I had to meet the homies by the baggage claim. When I retrieved my bag and stepped outside, I almost fainted in the hot ass sun. Just as I thought, the two niggas that were eyeing me were Nu'voe's people, Butch and Babywood.

"Aye, Chance!" The bigger one called out as I made my way towards them.

This nigga looked like the dude from the movie Green Mile. He was big and blacker than a motherfucker with a baldhead. The other nigga had a big ass nose.

"That's me," I replied.

"Welcome to Cali, my nigga. What's poppin', Damu?" the big nosed one said as we shook hands with our signature handshake and making our damu love official.

We hopped in a clean ass Camaro and pushed to the interstate.

"Gotta get you some Cali gear, homie," Babywood said as he fired up a big ass blunt and passed it back to me.

I hit that motherfucker and it felt like my lungs collapsed.

Cough-cough. "Goddamn-This-This that fire," I managed to say, damn near coughing up my lunch.

I pulled out my phone and called Lanise to check in with her, letting her know I was safe and sound. Next, I called Nu'voe's phone to let him know I was with the homies. He didn't answer so I left a message. Then I called Bianca. She answered the phone just as we pulled over.

"Hello," her voice came through the receiver.

"What's good, sexy?" I asked, smiling from ear-to-ear.

"Hey, Chance." she said back. "What's good, boo?"

"Hold on, B," I told her as I asked Green Mile where we were.

"Plaza Bonita Mall." he answered as he passed the blunt back to me.

We pulled into a parking spot.

"Hello. Yeah, I'm at the Plaza Bonita Mall, sexy,"

There was a silence before she spoke again.

"Wait a minute, you're here baby? Oh my God! When can I see you?" she asked with excitement.

"Umm, let me get settled at a nice room, and then I'm gonna call you. A'ight, baby?"

We made a set time we would be hooking up before we hung up. Once inside the mall, there wasn't a store we didn't tear up. The homies balled out for a nigga, showing that real West Coast love.

****

After a short drive, we pulled up into the hood. It looked like some real Menace 2 Society shit. I was just waiting for O-Dog to walk up. I can't front, I was a little shook not having my strap on. I was around a lot of strangers and the rumor in the feds was that West Coast Bloods don't fuck with the East Coast Bloods. I kept my mouth shut and my eyes open. I observed everything around me, looking for a rock or something just in case shit got ugly.

The sign read: BAY VISTA APARTMENTS. There were a bunch of kids running around and groups of people playing cards on their front porches. There were little cuties sitting on the steps and even a fucking weight bench!

We exited the car and I was amazed at how their hood looked. All these niggas were draped in green and I dug that because we rocked that green back home too. I was introduced to Lil' Face. I noticed him from the pictures that Nu'voe had hanging up in the cell. From the look on his face, I could tell he'll clap some shit if need be.

We shook hands. "Heard a lot about you," I said as we did another signature handshake.

"Same here," Lil' Face said in between pulls of his Newport. "I just spoke to 'Vo about an hour ago."

We chit-chatted about his uncle for a few moments before he disappeared into the crowd of people. I mingled with a few more homies until Gonzo was ready to go. They drove me to the strip and found me a nice suite at the Marriot. Babywood told me to relax and get comfortable then he'll be back shortly. They were taking me out for a night on the west coast. I still couldn't believe I was in California; gang bang capitol, the home of 64's, and Dickie suits. However, the reason I was there was far from good.

"This nigga really wants me to kill Treasure," I said to myself as I replayed our conversation. "Maybe I could change her mind not to snitch on my homie. Oh well, it is what it is."

I rolled a blunt of this Cali bud and within ten minutes flat, it felt like I was smoking Sherm.

"I gotta take some of this back home. I could get paid off this shit," I said out loud while staring at the half of blunt I'd laid in the ashtray.

I laid down and called Bianca to set a date and time to meet her at the salon. I couldn't wait to see my boo, and have the chance to holla at Treasure. This is going be some crazy shit.

CHAPTER EIGHT
DIAMOND

This triflin' ass bitch gonna do some shit like this to the nigga that's been taking good care of her ass since day one. *She doesn't appreciate shit!* I thought to myself. Diamond get a hold of ya self! You're too pretty to be stressing over some shit like this. I couldn't help but vent to myself while I was on the toilet, thinking about the fucked up shit Treasure was doing to Nu'voe. I wiped my pussy with a wet wipe, washed my hands, took my sexy ass back to my chair, and prepared to close the shop for the day. Bianca had left about an hour earlier so it was up to me to close up the shop.

What was crazy was that I always had been attracted to Nu'voe since the first day we met. I know he probably noticed my lustful eyes watching him on several occasions. One day we all went to the beach and I lied and told him I couldn't swim. The way he held me in his arms was just so comfortable. It was as if I belonged there. Not to mention I felt how hard his dick was as it pressed against my ass. Shit, I played with this pussy plenty of nights, thinking about him and what we could be if I got him away from her. Now look, she was getting ready to snitch on him. She was about to make that poor boy serve a hundred years, just because she couldn't take a little pressure. I was wondering if I could help. Maybe I could have gotten him a lawyer or something. My mother left me a nice piece of change. Helping him out would have been nothing to me.

I started snooping around Treasure's desk, hoping to find the address of the facility he was at. I wanted to write him. I locked the shop's doors and dimmed the lights just in case B or Treasure came back for some silly shit. I opened Treasure's desk and began my search. Let's see. I rummaged through her desk. Found nothing but condoms and a dildo at first. Freaky bitch. I couldn't even begin to imagine what was going on in her office while no one was around. Focusing on the task at hand, I stumbled upon a small book. Ok, what's this here, a diary? This bitch is still using a diary? I started flipping through the pages.

"The cops came to see me. Blah, blah. Last night Lil' face gave me the best dick I've ever had..." *Hold the fuck up,* I thought to myself, shocked by what I had read. *She fucking Nu'voe's nephew. She was a trifling little bitch.*

CHAPTER NINE
LIL' FACE

Damn! That's that east coast nigga my uncle was locked up with. I wondered what he was doing way out this way. I tried to figure out why the nigga was posted up with Babywood and Butch. He had to be trying to cop something. The nigga was fresh out of jail so I knew he was still on probation. He was either tough or he just wasn't right. Shit, whatever it was, my spider-senses were telling me to keep my eyes on that dude for real.

I had to holler at my uncle and see what the business was. I didn't know what was going on with me. Between Unk and Treasure, the shit was getting crazy and starting to fuck with me. Treasure was a beautiful woman and I started to catch feelings for her. Baby had her mind right, money right, and that pussy was on fire! If I told my uncle the truth, I wondered how he'd react to some shit like that. The nigga probably would cut me the fuck off. Nah, that's Unk. *He loves the shit out of me*, I thought to myself. Then on the other hand I had to be realistic. I did fuck his bitch.

My mind was trying to talk some sense into me. At that moment, I was tripping real hard. With the situation heavy on my mind, I continued to talk to myself. I had to ask myself what I would do if I found out some nigga was digging in my bottom bitch while I was gone. Shit, I'd knock the nigga and my bitch off while you bull-shitting.

"Ha, ha, ha," I had to laugh at myself.

Yeah, Unk was going to cut me the fuck off! Fuck that, I couldn't tell him about me and Treasure. I was just going to have to cut her off and bury that skeleton where it could never be found!

CHAPTER TEN
CHANCE

The feeling of someone tapping my leg woke me up. It was Babywood's big-nosed ass standing over me. Getting the cold out of my eyes, I looked at my watch.

"Damn, it's two in the morning! Shit!"

Babywood started laughing at me.

"Say, set ya clock back three hours. It's only twelve sum 'in'." he said while still laughing.

Yeah, a'ight mutha-fucka, I thought as I stood to my feet.

"Ayo, what the fuck was in that smoke? That shit had my heart beating fast and me sweating like Smokey in the chicken coop. I'm still high, bruh," I said in a serious tone.

This nigga looked at me, and simply said, "Welcome to California."

He flopped down on the couch.

I made my way to the bathroom to tighten up. I couldn't wait to see Bianca and hoped to beat that pussy up. I decided to call her and invite her to my room. Fuck it, I'll chill with the homies later.

"Yo, Blood!" I called out to Babywood getting his attention. "I need a thumper, bruh. Got this bitch coming through and you already know I'm outta bounds," I said as I entered the room.

"That's what I came over here for," he told me. "Here, take this."

He reached under his shirt and handed me a dusty silver Smith & Wesson .45.

50

I slid the clip out to check and make sure I had a full one before sliding the chamber back and popping one in the head. She was ready.

"Hollow points, huh?" I said out loud as I continued to inspect the fine piece of equipment. "This cool for now," I told him as I stuffed her in my top drawer.

Babywood looked on rather impressed at how I handled myself.

"Say homie, when you get done wit' the bitch, have her bring you through the Vista so I can get you some wheels. 'Vo still got some whips he left behind," he explained. "I'm sure she'll know where the Vista at," Babywood prepared to leave.

"A'ight homie. As soon as I'm done I'ma call you," I said as he exited the room.

Twenty minutes later, there was a knock at the door. I looked around making sure my shit was all good before opening the door. *Candles check, weed check, I smelled good , and I got the Patron on ice,* I thought to myself before I opened the door.

The sight before me took my breath away. "Oh shit," I mumbled under my breath.

This bitch was bad. She stood there with the prettiest smile I had ever seen. Giving her a once over, I couldn't help but take heed to the 6-inch, open-toed stiletto sandals, showing off her French tips. Her G-Star skinny leg jeans showed every curve on her body and she wore a regular white tank top with her nipples standing at full attention. Her lip-gloss was popping and her hair hung down showing her natural length.

We hugged real tight. "Hey, Chance," she whispered in my ear as we were stuck in our embrace.

She smelled so good. We broke our embrace and took a step back to stare at one another. "I can't believe you're here," she said with a smile. "Like, you really came all the way to Cali,"

If you only knew why, I thought to myself.

I let her in and we took our seats on the loveseat. We talked about everything under the sun from the reason behind me going to jail to Michael Jackson and Conrad Murray. We decided to watch a movie. I got on my soft shit and chose Love and Basketball on Netflix. We smoked a phat blunt of that Bin Laden and let the Patron do the talking. I couldn't help it but I know she caught me staring at them long ass legs. I'm a sucker for some pretty feet, a mean shoe game, and some sexy ass legs.

Vrrr! Vrrr!

The vibration of my phone caught both of our attention.

"You gonna answer that?" she asked, staring at me while licking her lips.

I knew it was Lanise, but the fucked up thing about it was that she was the last person on my mind at that point. I went to the nightstand to get my phone. Good thing was that Bianca knew I had a Shorty so she ain't trip. Seeing wifey come across my screen kind of made me nervous, and I know she peeped my body language.

"Hello," I spoke into the phone.

"Hey, bae. What you doing?" Lanise asked, in her one of a kind voice.

By just the way she sounded, I could tell she was lying on her stomach on my side of the bed with two fingers in that pussy. One thing was for sure, she had no problem getting herself off.

"Shit, just enjoying the California scenery," as soon as I said that Bianca popped her titties out of her shirt.

She began licking her lips then sucked her own nipples. She motioned for me to come here with her finger.

"I miss you, baby" Lanise said, and then there was a brief silence. "Hello-Hello! Baby, what are you doing?" she asked, raising her voice.

I heard her but I couldn't speak. Bianca had me stuck in a trance. Her pants had come completely off and she was doing a strip tease, grabbing her ankles and making her ass clap.

"Heeelloooo!" Lanise screamed into the phone.

Saying what came to mind, "I'm sorry, bae. This weed got me stuck. I'm trippin'. I love you, baby. Hit'chu in the morning."

I hung up the phone without giving her a chance to say anything. I turned the phone off and enjoyed the show.

Bianca stood tall, ass shaking and all. The way she stared at me fucked up my train of thought. She dropped to her hands and knees and began to crawl towards me. By then I'd grew harder than a role of quarters. I was on straight penitentiary shit with a pair of sweatpants and a grey tank top on. I came out of that shit so fast. I was like Superman in his prime.

She knelt before me, looking up at me with them sexy ass cat eyes. I watched her take my dick out my boxer briefs, and then she took me all the way in her mouth. On some real shit, a nigga holding some heavy artillery under the hood. When this bitch took my whole dick in her mouth I was sold. My toes curled and my stomach got tight. Yeah, I would've tricked the whole bank on this bitch. She worked her head from side-to-side, back and forth, slow then fast, then slow again. She sucked dick like a fat girl. She came up for air, and then pushed me on the bed. We got in a 69 position. She had the prettiest little pussy; shaved bald, smelled good, and tasted even better.

Damn, Chance. You trippin' eating another bitch's pussy. My inner voice kept repeating itself but I sucked harder- and-harder on her clit until her juices spilled on my face. What about ya wifey? I asked myself again. I shook that shit off and watched her swallow my first nut without stopping one time. This was going to be a long night.

TWO HOURS LATER...

We showered together after a mean four round fuck session. She was a mean combo. Not only was she pretty but she had some good head and some good pussy. *Damn, I was tripping.*

After our shower I went to the closet and pulled out my Oakland A's jersey, matching fitted, a pair of denim ash washed Sean John jeans with a touch of green going down the seams, and a pair of beef & broccoli Timbs with a V-neck under my top. I put my .45 on my waistline, rolled me a blunt, and then Bianca and I rolled out. We stopped at Fat Burger's, smoked another blunt, and then headed to the Bay Vista projects. When we pulled up it was popping outside. It was jammed pack with people of all likes. She found a parking spot and exited the car. I could tell niggas were on point from how they eyed the car.

Babywood approached and came to my rescue.

"He bool y'all!" Babywood shouted.

From the looks of things, he had a lot of pull around there because niggas went right back to what they were doing.

Bianca and I sat on the hood of her Nissan Maxima just kicking it until Butch pulled up in a clean ass 1987 Cutlass Supreme.

"Damn that mutha-fucka nice," I said to myself.

He revved the engine, bringing the dual pipes to life as he killed the engine.

"What's happening?" he asked as we shook hands with our signature. He eyed Bianca before he spoke, "Who dis, Blood?"

The way he looked at her, I instantly became mad. She looked him up and down and sucked her teeth.

"I'm with him," she said, wrapping her arms into mines.

As he was about to respond, someone yelled out, "Skyline Niggas!"

I instinctively pushed Bianca out the way as I remembered the stories Nu'voe told me about the war between Lincoln and the Skyline. It's just like back home how homies beef with homies.

"Chance, what's going on?" Bianca asked when she saw me pull my strap.

In that very moment, shots rang out.

Blatt! Blatt! Blatt!

I was in the middle of some Boyz N Da Hood shit as I dropped to one knee trying to locate where the bullets were coming from. It was a beat up looking Bonneville creeping down the street; it was about yards from where I was, heading in my direction.

"Chance, let's go!" Bianca called out as she had already jumped in her driver's seat.

Fuck this shit, I thought to myself as I hurried behind the wheel of Butch's Cutlass. The keys were still in the ignition. I fired up the engine, slapped it in reverse, and slammed on the gas pedal. My timing was perfect. I slammed into the passenger's side of the Bonneville, causing them to run into a parked car. They were stuck. With my adrenaline pumping, I jumped out the car and aimed at the three people who occupied the car. I emptied the clip into the car, crushing everything that stood in my .45's way. The homies were right behind me and they began to put so many holes in that car that I even started to feel sorry for the people inside.

"Chance, come on!" Bianca screamed at the top of her lungs.

Sirens could be heard from afar. Not wanting to make Butch a suspect by leaving his car at the scene, I jumped back in the Cutlass.

"Go-Go-I'll follow you!" I shouted.

The Maxima sped away as I burned rubber right on her bumper. The rear fender was banged up, but I still managed to get the fuck up out of there.

CHAPTER ELEVEN
NU'VOE

The vibration from my cell phone woke me up. It was 5 o'clock in the morning Midwest time so that meant it was 3:00 a.m. in San Diego.

Why the fuck is somebody calling me this goddamn early in the morning? I thought as I jumped up off of my bunk and grabbed the phone. When I looked at the phone, I recognized the number. It was my nigga, Babywood.

"What's poppin', Wood?" I asked, knowing that something had to be going on for him to be calling me this early.

"You know flowers," he responded.

"Is that ree-zite?" I replied.

"Yeah dat. Ta-zoo nee-zite, ya-bee-zoy," Babywood explained.

"Ha-zoo?" I asked.

"Cree-zoss tee-zownas kee-zame three-zoo and ya-bee-zoy gee-zot dee-zown," Babywood described what happened as he talked in our signature language.

Ever since we were teenagers, we had our own language so that we could talk to each other and nobody would understand us but us.

"Vo?"

"What's up?"

"The bee-zoy is o-fee-zicial. No hesitation at ee-zall."

"Yeah I know. That's why he's out there, and make sure he's safe and looked out for. I'm gonna need him."

"You already know. I got 'em, 'Vo. Enough said," Babywood insured me that he would look out for Chance while he was in San Diego.

"Alright Wood good lookin'. I'ma holla atcha later."

"One."

As I hung up the phone, I thought, Damn, this nigga ain't been in the town two days and already done caught a body. If he kept that shit up, he wasn't going to be able to do what I needed him to do. Then my thoughts went to Treasure. I looked at the phone, and then at her picture that was taped to my mirror. That's when I decided to call her. She answered on the third ring.

"Hello."

"Hey sexy, girl," I spoke in a hushed but seductive voice.

"Nu'voe, what you doing? And how you calling me right now?" Treasure asked.

She was curious about how I was calling her straight through and at that hour. My joking side came out so I decided to have a little fun.

"I'm out that's how. Go to the window and look down," I said, playing with her and seeing how she would react.

It sounded like she had gotten off the phone.

"Hello, Treasure?" I asked and there was no answer. I yelled her name into the phone. "Treasure!"

This time she responded, "Why you playin', Nu'voe? You know how much I miss you and want you home!" Treasure spoke with a little attitude in her voice.

Then why is your name on the D.A.'s list to be a witness, I thought. The whole thing about Treasure being a witness against me had been eating me up so I decided to address the situation head on.

NO TRUSTPASSING

"Treasure, there's somethin' that's been bothering me, and I feel that you and I need to talk about it."

Dinnnngaling! Dinnnngaling! Dinnnngaling!

"What the fuck!"

You had to be kidding me. The fucking phone had died on me. Now how the fuck am I supposed to charge this mutha-fucka back up.

Closing the phone, I thought back on my life and all the things I'd been through. I had never been faced with life in prison, and now that I was it was scary. Truth be told, I've always been considered a hard nigga, but when my lawyer told me I could get life in prison I was shook. Especially when I saw Treasure's name as the key witness.

See, I came up from nothing. You know, piecing up on a dime sack of weed as a knucklehead just so me and the homies could get high. Then I found out that being broke wasn't the thing to be. Instead of smoking dimes, I started selling them. Eventually I moved up to quarters, halves, and wholes. I never really was the cocaine type of dude and stuck to weed. With the help of a few connections, I was able to turn my dirty money, clean and invest in a couple of businesses. Going from ashy to classy. I'll tell you one thing, if God got me out of the life sentence; I swear I would be done with the bullshit. I hoped Treasure's name being on that list was a mistake because if it wasn't, it's going to kill me to have to kill her.

CHAPTER TWELVE
TREASURE

"Hello, Hello!" I said into the phone. "Did this nigga hang up on me?" I asked out loud, still stuck for two reasons.

For one, this nigga called me from a cell phone, and I knew he was probably fucking one of them C.O. bitches, or got one of them Kansas bitches moving out for him. I had to check myself because I was mad at him for making moves behind the wall while I was out here fucking his nephew. Silly me. Then secondly, he said he had to talk to me about something that was bothering him. I prayed that he wasn't about to ask me about that 30-page statement I made on him. The feds told me they would seal my name, and he would never know it was me. He would think it was one of his boys. It couldn't have been that so I wondered what he was talking about.

"Long legs, red bottoms!" blared through my cellphone as my Trina ringtone told me Bianca was reaching out.

It was 3:26 a.m. What the hell could she possibly want this late?

"What's up, B?" I asked.

She began screaming and talking so fast that it was like she was high on something.

"B, slow down girl and talk to me!" I yelled through the speaker.

"Treasure! Girl, I just seen some wild shit over in the Vista!"

I had to take a moment to think before I spoke.

"What the hell you doing over there?" I asked, already knowing her hot ass was somewhere chasing dick.

"I was with Chance!" she said with excitement.

The whole conversation seemed to pause after she said she was with Chance. I hooked her up with Nu'voe's best friend in jail a while back, but I knew that he was from Jersey and was shocked to hear he was way out here. What the fuck is he doing in Cali? I thought to myself.

"Girl, he shot these niggas that was creeping," Bianca started to explain. "But it was how he did it. He was so smooth and had so much swagger when he was doing it. Shit, my pussy is so wet right now just thinking about that shit."

I had to ask, "What is Chance doing out here?"

She totally disregarded my question.

"Fuck all that. Treasure, this nigga dicked me so good in the back seat of the car he did the shooting in, but earlier we got it in at the hotel. Girl, he busts my ass!"

"So where is he now?" I asked her horny ass.

"He's at his hotel room. I'll go get him in the morning so I can get him a rental so he can have sum'in' to drive around in. Then we coming to the shop to see you. I forgot to tell you that he wanted to see you and sum'in' about the shop," Bianca said.

She told me everything but how much hair Chance had on his ass. After we hung up I called that number Nu'voe called me from but got no answer. Nu'voe wanted to talk to me about something but what was it?

All that sex talk Bianca was telling me kind of got me a little hot. There was a picture Nu'voe sent me that I kept on the nightstand. I stared at it and began to please myself with my two fingers. Bad thing was he wasn't in the picture alone.

CHAPTER THIRTEEN
LIL' FACE

I tried my hardest but I couldn't continue to listen to Babywood and Butch go on about how this nigga Chance killed E-Money and his squad. Crazy thing was that E-Money was an across town nigga that the turf had been funkin' with for years. Chance was the nigga to put him out of his misery. Ever since the homie Bubba Cheeks passed away it had been an all-out war zone. The nigga Chance got praise because he let his gun do the talking.

I wanted to call Treasure but that would only lead to one thing, me fucking her. Damn and Bianca was looking good too and had the nerve to be all hugged up with that East Coast nigga. First chance I got, I was going to stamp his ass. Something wasn't right about dude. I could smell it.

I gave Babywood, Butch, and the rest of the homies dap before I rolled out. My mind was elsewhere and I needed something to smoke. I drove to the sherm spot and copped me a double dip, then drove through the Southside and picked up Patrice a.k.a. Mouth-Piece. She was a Spanish chick who was thick in the thighs with big titties and an ass to die for. She was a prostitute, but she was going to be my Beyoncé for the evening.

After a little small talk, I found somewhere to park that was real quiet. Long story short, she sucked me whole while I puffed on my sherm stick. I was so high because halfway through I swear that bitch's face transformed to J-Lo's.

CHAPTER FOURTEEN
DIAMOND

Dear Nu'voe,

I know you're wondering why I'm writing you, but there's a number of reasons. One is because Treasure is no good for you. She's trifling, disloyal, selfish, and most of all a RAT BITCH! Yeah, you read it right. She sold you out to the fed's and now you're looking at life fuckin' wit' this bitch. I can help. My father knows a lot of the top dogs in the federal building. Plus, when my mother died I got a nice piece of money so I can put up whatever you need. I'll do whatever, and plus I have the biggest crush on you :). Ray Charles could see that I was on you, Boo! I never told anyone this but one night you came to Treasure house before y'all moved in together and you were pissy drunk. She went to get something to eat and well, I undressed you and helped myself to a taste. You probably thought I was Treasure when we got in a 69, and you ate this pussy and came in my mouth.

The sound of Bianca and Treasure's voice alarmed me so I had to end my letter and look like I was busy.

"Hey, Diamond," they both said in unison.

"Hey," I said in a real dry tone.

It was hard for me to move because the memory of Nu'voe's dick in my mouth had my pussy soaking wet.

"Diamond, Diamond!" Treasure yelled, waking me out of my trance.

If only she knew what I was thinking about.

"Yeah, I'm good. Just a little tired that's all," I said, dismissing her.

I strutted to the closet to grab some supplies when I overheard Bianca saying something about a shootout she witnessed and some nigga named Chance.

I still couldn't help but think about Nu'voe and somehow my right hand found its way to my wet pussy. The door was slightly opened and the thrill of getting caught by Bianca, Treasure, or a customer only drove my fingers deeper into my clit.

"Ooh, umm, shit," I moaned as my knees began to buckle.

I pulled my Ms60's skirt up a little higher with my free hand and pushed my fingers deeper into my pussy. I envisioned Nu'voe's drunken dick going in and out of my mouth. I could feel his tongue press against my pussy and ass. Before I knew it I had come all over my fingers. I leaned against the wall to get myself together.

Deciding to get kinkier, I took my cu

m stained fingers and smeared it all over Nu'voe's letter so he can get a whiff of how good this pussy smells. As I made my way to my desk, I felt Treasure and Bianca staring at me. Maybe they heard me. I grabbed my Y.S.L. clutch along with his letter tucked inside.

"Be right back, I'm going to the post office and then the Western Union," I said, hoping Treasure would catch what I was saying.

I walked out, putting an extra step on my Alexander McQueen peep toe pumps, throwing my 40-inch ass from side-to-side. I looked back and locked eyes with Treasure, just like I knew she would be watching me.

CHAPTER FIFTEEN
NU'VOE

I was up in medical scrubbing the hell out of my dick! This morning after the phone died on me I had to figure out how to charge the motherfucker back up. The only way I knew how was to go find the nurse broad that Chance got the phone from. I don't know why I didn't think about how I was going to charge the phone back up ahead of time.

So when the police unlocked my door and I heard pill call over the loudspeaker, I did my one, two and slid up to medical. I was there for fifteen minutes until Ms. Burnes finally noticed me. When she did, she put all of her other appointments on hold then called my name.

"Mr. Davoe, come with me."

The reason why I know she put her other appointments on hold was because I never had an appointment to see the nurse or the doctor. It was as if she was waiting on me or something. Ms. Burnes led me to an unoccupied room and closed the door behind us.

"About time!" she said with an attitude as she frowned up her face. "I thought I was going to have to put you on call-out," she added.

The call-out was a piece of paper that all inmates were required to check every day because on any given day your name might pop up on there, letting you know that you are being summoned.

Looking at Ms. Burnes, I got straight to the point.

"Look, I need the charger to the phone. The bitch died on me last night."

"That's not a problem," she replied and started to unbutton her scrub top.

"What you doin'?" I asked.

"What do you mean, what am I doing? Don't you need something? Well, I do to." By the time she was done with her reply, her top was wide open.

The sight I saw disgusted me.

"What you waiting on?" she barked at me.

I had been locked up for years without having a piece of pussy. Every nigga in here was deprived of that luxury. Some of us were strong when it came to controlling the wild beast known as hormones. I'm afraid to say that some of us fell short when it came to that. For instance, some niggas walked around with holes in the pockets of their khaki pants so that they could jack off to the women C.O.'s and education workers. The icing on the cake is the gangsta-ass niggas sword fighting with these punks. The shit is ridiculous!

All bullshit aside, I weighed my options and thought; I really need that phone charged up. Plus, it's just me and her. Ain't nobody gonna know nothin', and I ain't had no pussy in years! My mind was already made up.

"Davoe," she said, "I know all about you, your case, and that bitch that's telling on you. I can help you if you want me to. I know a lawyer who will be willing to work your case for a little bit of nothing. Just help me and I will do whatever it takes to help you. I promise!"

When she was done talking, I felt like Shallow Hal. My vision was manipulated by her words and promises. When I had walked into the room with her she was big as a house weighing every bit of 300 pounds. However, right now she was looking like a Victoria's Secret supermodel. Swallowing my pride, my reputation, and my morals I attacked Ms. Burnes with the fervor of a desperate man. When I placed my face in between her breast, she wrapped both of her arms around me. The feeling I felt wasn't that bad. I had never been with a fat woman before, but her hold was comforting. I was unsure what it was. It might have been the fact that I hadn't felt a woman's touch in who knows how long, and to tell you the truth it felt damn good. Ms. Burnes pushed away from me and with the agility I thought a woman her size couldn't possibly possess she hopped on top of one of the operating tables. She pulled her scrub bottoms down and spread her legs.

"Come get it, big boy," she said in her sexy voice.

Lying on her back, her oversized titties drooped to the side and her body showcased rolls of fat. When I looked down, to my surprise my dick was hard as a rock! So much for self-control.

Get that charger boy, but most importantly get that lawyer and get home. My mind talked to me with such clarity and for the next 20 minutes I held up Ms. Burnes stomach and fucked the charger and my freedom out of her. Once I was done, reality immediately hit me in the face. I pulled up my pants and had to run to the bathroom because after I nutted and looked at Ms. Burnes fat ass, my stomach felt like it did a project back flip. I had to throw up. I ran straight to the bathroom.

This shit better work, I thought as I held the charger in my hand. To think, Chance was hitting that on a regular. That nigga was nastier than a mutha-fucka! I ain't tripping though. This is just one more skeleton in the closet for me. I couldn't tell anybody about that one. Treasure would kill a nigga.

Before I scrubbed a layer of skin off, I got up out of there and headed back to my cell.

My thoughts were all over the place, but mainly focused on Treasure. She was my baby, my everything. She was the one I wanted to have my babies, but the information my lawyer showed me told me that she didn't feel the same way. Even though I saw it with my own eyes, I didn't want to believe it. I wasn't going to believe it. I was in love and as we all know; love can be a blinding thing.

CHAPTER SIXTEEN
CHANCE

Shit got way too crazy the other night. My first night in the West and I was putting my murder game down already. What the fuck were they thinking, I wasn't going to bust my gun or something? It was all good though. I was all the way in with them after that. This nigga Babywood had to make something happen with this money. I needed at least half before I blew Treasure's brains out. Bianca, copped me a Buick Lacrosse rental to get me back and forth. I quickly got dressed because it was time to meet Treasure and I had to make a good impression on the bitch I was getting paid to kill. I dressed in a pair of Buffalo denim loose fit jeans, black and white Prada sneakers, and one of my fitted V-necks to show off the build.

I hopped in my rental and let the navigation system direct me to Treasure's shop. When I pulled up I was impressed by the layout. Even though 'Vo showed me million flicks of it, the shop looked better in person. When I stepped foot in the salon Bianca made sure she met me by the door, letting all the customers know who I belonged toc. Funny how chicks love to mark their territory and she was looking even better than the last time I saw her.

"Hey, boo," she smiled as she slid her tongue down my throat.

I loved every second of it. As we broke our embrace, I had a chance to see all the eye candy that sat before me. From what I could see, I was the topic of conversation at the moment. Eyes were being cut at me, and the body language was obvious.

"Is that Chance, Bianca?" a female's voice called out.

I looked in the direction of the voice and when I laid eyes on Treasure I almost fainted. Don't get me wrong, Bianca was a bad bitch, but Treasure was a fucking angel sent from above. I replayed all the pictures I have seen of her, including all the thong shots, but nothing compared to this face-to-face encounter.

"What's up, Chance?" she asked as she hugged me.

Now this wasn't the, hey you're my man's old celly or you're the nigga he sent to kill me, kind of hug. This was a, where have you been all my life, kind of hug.

I inhaled her scent and my nose flared up. She led me to her office and we talked about Nu'voe for about an hour. Bianca's next appointment showed up so Treasure decided to take me to the other establishments. We jumped in her cocaine white CL550 Benz and pulled off. As I was taking in the sights and nodding my head to The Game joint booming through the speaker, Treasure turned down the system causing me to look her way.

"What are you really doing out here?" she asked, totally catching me off guard.

I had to think fast.

With a slight smile, I simply replied, "Okay, Nu'voe sent me out here to audit the books on the shops to make sure all the T's are crossed and the I's are dotted, feel me?" What I was really thinking about the whole time I spoke was blowing the brains out of that pretty rat bitch. "I took some accountant classes and I know my shit so the feds can't fuck with you if they decide to get slick," I continued.

I threw the word feds out there to get a reaction out of her and just like I suspected she became paranoid.

"So, he doesn't trust me?" she asked as she became upset. "He sent you out here to trace my steps!"

"Wait, wait," I said, trying to regain control of the situation. "It's not like that, Shorty. He just sent you a little defense to protect you, that's all. Consider me a lineman and you're the quarterback. I'm here to make sure not a hair on ya pretty lil' head gets touched, feel me?" As I finished my sentence tears began to form in the corners of her eyes. "You ok?" I asked.

"Yeah, I just miss him that's all. You being here is just making me think of him. I'm sorry for this."

She got herself together as I finished taking in the sights of San Diego. The trees were beautiful and the atmosphere was different. I thought about reaching under my shirt and at the next stop light blowing this bitch's noodle loose. Then my phone vibrated in my pocket.

JUSTIN came across my screen. I chose not to answer. I'll deal with him later.

When she pulled over in front of the rim shop there were all sorts of people loitering around. All types of exotic rims hung along the walls, 20's, 30's, you name it, and they had it. As we stepped in we were greeted by a nice looking dark skinned chick.

"Hey, Treasure," she eyed me as she spoke, unsure if Treasure was with me or not.

"How you doing?" I jumped right in as she smiled, showing a pearly white set of teeth.

"Hello to you too," she shot right back.

Treasure pulled me by the arm while she was laughing.

"Bianca gonna kick ya ass," she told the dark skinned chick.

I couldn't help but laugh because once the girl heard Bianca's name she got the fuck away from me.

"The office is back here," she said as I followed closely behind her watching the Gucci sign on her jeans disappear with every step she took.

She must have sensed it because she stopped dead in her tracks and bent over like she dropped something.

She shouldn't play like that. I walked into her and my hands were all over the place.

"Oh shit. Excuse me, my bad." I said as I backed away from her, but the smirk on her face just confirmed my suspicion.

I looked over the store's records and bank statements until a tap on the door broke my train of thought. Babywood stepped in.

"Oh shit. What's good, Damu?" he said, smiling from ear-to-ear. "Say, that was some real shit you put down last night, homie. That's the type shit I'm talking about. I hollered at 'Vo about that too."

"Ain't 'bout nothin', homie," I reclined back in the office chair. "Real niggas do real things. But fuck all that, I need to holla' atcha for a second."

"Hold on, bruh," he said as he passed Treasure a plastic bag of money, which she put inside the mid-sized safe behind the desk.

My palms grew sweaty and I contemplated reaching for my heater. I was still desperate for money. I wondered how much was in there.

I understood why she was caught up. She had this nigga bringing money straight from the trap to her place of business and that's a no-no!

She excused herself and Babywood and I both found ourselves staring at her while she left. I wasted no time.

"Yo, Wood, what's up with that bread?" I asked him, cutting straight to the chase.

The look he gave me just sealed his fate.

"Homie, you gotta holla at "Vo. He ain't telling me to give you shit, and until he does, I'm not giving you shit."

Boom!

I envisioned his head exploding from the force of the .45 on my waistline.

"So you telling me he never told you to give me no money?" I asked for the sake of clarity.

"Nah, Blood," he said just as Treasure walked back in the office.

CHAPTER SEVENTEEN
LANISE

This nigga Chance must really think I was born yesterday. I'm supposed to be his wifey, but he was out there in Cali fucking around on me. I was the one there for him all those years. Shit, I was filling my pussy up with balloons of weed, dope, and whatever he asked for and this is how he repaid me?

Okay, so yeah I was out here fucking like Pinky the porn star off her period but so what. I wasn't supposed to get mine while he was gone all those years. At least I had the abortions and didn't have any babies while he was gone. Yeah, I violated but to be honest, his father eats way better pussy then he does.

One night I was stressing over Chance's ass, and then next thing you know I was riding his father reverse cowgirl in his wheelchair.

On another night, I was putting this fire ass head on him while he worked a dildo in and out my ass. I had his old ass talking in tongues with his toes curling.

Next thing you know he blurted out, "I know where my son hides his money!"

At first I thought the head had him tripping, but turns out he was on point.

Then he met him a white chick and just like a typical man, his nose was wide open. I argued with him over money. I had to suck him off just to get a few Gs. It was hard out here for me. So now who's stupid? He should have read the signs: NO TRUST PASSING!

CHAPTER EIGHTEEN
CHANCE

I talked to Treasure for another half hour or so until Bianca came to pick me up. Right then I was contemplating on robbing that rim shop blind. I mind fucked Treasure so good she told me what day she makes the drops to the bank. I made up some excuse about needing to know the routine of the money flow, and the silly bitch fell for it. From checking her books, I could see why Nu'voe was in the position he was in. He left one hell of a paper trail and all the money has two names on it, his and hers.

Bianca and I enjoyed each other's time, and then she dropped me off to get my car. We made plans to go half on a baby later. When I got back to the room, I put my plan in motion to kill two dogs in one fight like Michael Vick. I had something for their asses.

TWO DAYS LATER...

I flew Justin in from Jersey and took him to meet Bianca and her friend Desire. Then I took him through the projects and he loved everything about California. The clock read 1:38a.m.

"Let's do this," I said as we approached the rim shop.

In less than 20 seconds, we were able to bypass the bullshit ass Walmart padlock. Once inside, we headed straight to the safe and removed it from its place. I memorized the combination on the Digi-safe: 26-13-99-16.

Click!

We quickly packed a duffel bag with all the contents in the safe then proceeded to hit the drawers. The first part of my plan was done. I took the red spray paint out of my back pocket and spray painted SKYLINE EASTSIDE PIRU all over the place to cause some beef and motive.

We made our way to the car. I popped the trunk and dropped the keys by accident. Justin reached down to grab them for me.

Whack!

I smacked him across the head and he was out cold. I restarted the stolen Chevy Lumina and drove off with Justin in the trunk.

I drove to the same spot Bianca showed me to dump Butches Cutlass. It was a secluded area that sat alongside a riverbank. I pulled over to pop the trunk, and Justin was still out cold. I removed the duffel bag and transferred the contents to a smaller bag so I wouldn't look suspicious. I nudged him with the butt of the gun until he woke up. He rolled over and opened his eyes.

"What the fuck, man? Ayo, Chance what you doing, homie?" he pleaded for his life as he stared at me with the gun in my hand aimed at him.

"Same thing you did to me," I said in a hushed tone.

Not wanting to drag this out any longer, I put seven fireballs in his face and chest.

I put the car in neutral and let it roll into the river.

"Fuck that grimy ass lil' nigga."

The hotel I was staying at was about two miles away so I decided to stroll and enjoy the nice 85 degree weather. A smooth getaway.

****

The next morning my sleep was disturbed by the constant ringing of my phone. It was Treasure.

"Hello," I answered half asleep.

"Chance, come to the shop. I need you!"

I could tell she had been crying.

"A'ight, I'm on my way."

When I arrived the cops were taking pictures and asking questions. One person in authority stood out the most. He was wearing some Levi's jeans, a crew shirt, and a buzz cut. He looked like the feds to me. He didn't talk much. He just kept his eyes on Treasure. Damn, what has she gotten herself into?

Then, thirty minutes later, we were at the rim shop alone.

"Are you okay?" I asked her with a look of concern.

"Can we just get outta here? I have to get away from here," she said then she began to cry again.

Then out of nowhere I just blurted out, "The hotel I'm staying at has some good room service."

I just had to think of a way to get her alone so I could kill the bitch and get back to Lanise. We chilled in my room and smoked some bomb ass weed Treasure pulled from her purse. We ordered some lasagna in meat sauce with a side of Caesar's salad, long island ice teas, and some cheesecake. She was extremely quiet, and that's when I noticed she was crying again.

"Treasure, you good?" I asked as I slid over to comfort her.

"Yeah-Yeah, I'm good. It's just—."

"Ssshh," I calmed her down and put my finger to her lips. "I know what you're goin' through and I know how you feel. All the stress, cops harassing you, and you're afraid."

She melted with every word I spoke. I was trying to get her to confess so that I wouldn't feel bad about killing her.

"It's hard, Chance. It's so fucking hard," she said with her head in her hands. "I just don't know what to do. I'm not used to this life. I never had to worry about—" She paused. I knew it was coming. "Chance, they came and talked to me-

I-I gave them information about Nu'voe-Then-I got caught lying to them," she stuttered before she broke all the way down.

"Chance, they had pictures of me going to the bank, at the car dealership, coded phone calls and I just panicked," she said between her tears.

In the midst of her crying, when I went to reach out to her, I spilled the pasta sauce all over myself.

"Shit!"

I got up to go to the bathroom to clean myself up. I stared at myself in the mirror, and I knew what had to be done. I can get her in the car and take her to the spot where I left Justin stinking. That's what I decided to do.

I exited the bathroom with my shirt off. The look she gave me stopped me in my tracks.

"You a'ight?" I asked.

"Can you get me some tissue, please?"

Doing what she asked, I retrieved some tissue off the roll and made my way back to where she was. When I looked up there she stood asshole naked.

"Do you think what I did was wrong, Chance?" she asked as she took baby steps towards me.

I was stuck on her beauty. Damn, she was bad and the bulge in my pants showed that John Shotty felt the same way.

"Am I wrong for what I did?" she asked me again.

We stood face-to-face. Her nipples were pressed against my bare chest and I couldn't speak. She opened her mouth and we kissed. Her arms found their way around my neck. My hands fell to her ass and I pulled her close. The connection was there and we both felt it.

We didn't make it to the bed. Instead we went to the bathroom. With both hands around her waist, I lifted her onto the sink. I had to taste her, and I had to feel her insides. Her clean, shaved pussy smelled like roses and tasted like candy yams. She put both of her hands on my baldhead and drove me to her spot. I licked and flicked my tongue around her clit until she released not one but two nuts on my face.

After I was done tasting her juices, I bent her over the sink and entered her from the back. We stared at one another through the mirror, and it was something about looking at our own reflection that made me fuck her harder. From the way she was tossing it back I could tell she felt the same way.

"Damn-Chance-You feel so-So good," she moaned as I watched all nine inches of me disappear inside of her.

Her pussy was so wet that the inside of my thighs were soaked. I slapped her on her ass and pulled her hair, which took her to new heights.

"Ahh shit! Right there! Fuck me harder!"

I pushed in as deep as I could, and she took every bit of me.

She looked back and licked her lip, and then said, "Dis pussy good? Huh? Fuck ya boy's wifey-That's right! Fuck me how I need it,"

She moaned and grunted then did the unthinkable. She took me out her drenched pussy and put me in her ass.

Then 45 minutes later we laid in the Jacuzzi with her back pressed against my chest. I stared at the ceiling, feeling bad for what I was about to do. Nu'voe was my nigga and Lanise was my bitch. I couldn't forget about Bianca because I was feeling her like no other, but at that moment, Mr. Shotty and I agreed, Fuck Nu'voe! Treasure is my bitch now.

CHAPTER NINETEEN
NU'VOE

I woke up with one of them attitudes that said "Don't fuck wit' me!"

It had been like that for a few weeks. The fucking phone that Chance left me kept dying on me so something must have been wrong with the battery. Every time I looked at the call out list my name was on that bitch! It was medical that kept putting my name on the list. I knew it had to be Ms. Burnes' fat ass. She was out of her rabbit ass mind if she thought I was going to keep swiping her down and fighting back vomit just to charge up the phone.

She had a nigga like me fucked up for real. The more I thought about it, the more I felt like she had been playing me. I had been waiting on the bitch to get at me about the lawyer she was talking about, but I hadn't heard anything. I was starting to think that nothing had even been said. I had to admit the bitch had game. She worked me out of some dick.

Another reason why I was mad at the world was because of the bullshit ass indictment these fed motherfuckers slapped on me out of nowhere. I was fourteen months to the house, then bam! What type of shit was that? I couldn't win for losing.

Then the letters that I received last night had me up all night tossing and turning. I swear to God I've never had this much bad luck in my life.

I was upstairs listening to Jay-Z and Kanye West's new CD, Watch the Throne, when one of my partners tapped me on my shoulder, and said, "Aye Nu'voe, the counselor in the unit lookin' fa you. I think its legal mail, homie."

The mentioning of legal mail did something crazy to me. Ever since I fired my lawyer and hired a jailhouse lawyer to handle my case, I had been on eggshells waiting on some type of response from the courts. The 3 p.m. yard recall bell sounded and I B-lined it to the counselor's office.

"Mr. White, you got mail fo' me," I said as more of a statement rather than a question.

Counselor White looked up and was about to respond before he noticed the desperation on my face.

Instead, he took a deep breath and a couple of seconds to gather the right words to talk, and said, "I see you've been waiting on this. Good luck."

He opened the big manila envelope in front of me and had me sign for it. As I was headed to my cell, I noticed the unit mail call list was posted up. I scanned through it and saw that Rm. 249 had mail, small and big. *About time*, I thought.

I had been waiting on my Urban Ink magazine and some panty shots from this little stripper bitch I was in contact with before I got locked up. When I got the mail, the Urban Ink magazine was there but the panty shots were missing in action, and replaced by three letters from Treasure, Chance, and my nigga Babywood.

"Fuck that lyin' bitch. These were the people that really had love for me."

It was damn near count time. So I turned it in to my cell with my letters, changed clothes, and prepared myself to read my love from the streets.

The first letter I opened up was Treasure's. Who the fuck else letter was I supposed to open up first? Her letter made me feel my situation. It made me hate my situation. Her letter made me mad at myself and mad at the world. It made me cry.

To the only man I truly know, love, and always will belong too! First, I want to say that I love you! You were my everything. You showed me how to love. You gave me strength. You were also the father that I never had. Nu'voe, you were my rock but at the same time you left me out here by myself. Just like my father left me, just like everything else in my life that I loved!

As I'm sure you know the police have been harassing me day in and day out. Nu'voe, they're threatening to put me in jail for the rest of my life. Instead of me continuing to live this lie, I've decided to come clean with you. Nu'voe, yes I love you, but I'm not willing to spend the rest of my life in jail for a man that left me by myself. I'm sorry, Nu'voe, but I'm going to be a witness against you. Please don't hold it against me, but I don't know what else to do. If you wouldn't have left me, none of this would have ever happened!

P.S.

I'll always love you!

TREASURE

P.S.S.

By the way, I got the message you sent through Chance!

Once I read the P.S.S. part of the letter I knew something was wrong. Treasure wasn't supposed to know that I had sent Chance out there for her. *What the fuck was going on?* I thought to myself. I re-read the letter three times and each time my heart ached even more. I tossed the letter on my locker and grabbed the letter from Babywood.

Nu'voe, what's poppin', homie? I'm just reachin' out to my G. Check it out, that cat out this way was speakin' on that bree-zed real slee-zick and that shee-zit didn't see-zit too wee-zel wit' mee-

zee, and to tee-zel yee-zoo the truth I don't tree-zust ya bee-zoy foree-zel it's somethin' bee-zout his eez-eyes.

Not only that, the shop on Market got robbed and whoever hit it knew what they were doin'. No rims were taken, no pumps, or switches, the niggas went straight to the safe and had the combination. They took everything! $237 thousand. 'Vo the shop ain't never got hit since it's been open. Now this east coast nigga's out here and then this. He came to the shop right befo' it got hit to talk to me about that bree-zed. Somethin' ain't right 'Vo.

Check it out, I wasn't gonna tell you but you my pat'nah fo' life 'Vo, the nigga been up under Treasure real tough like lately and I mean tough. The shit looks real funny to me, homie. What you want me to do? Holla back and let me know. One love! Head up and Chest out!

Ya nigga, Babywood

"Yeah, Wood I sent the nigga out there to get up under her so she would change her mind. I hope the shit works. The nigga Chance is a good nigga, Wood," I said, talking to myself out loud.

Babywood didn't know that I was being superseded indicted and that Treasure was set to be the key witness against me. If Babywood knew that Treasure's days would surely be numbered, and I couldn't have that. I still loved her. If only I could talk to her face-to-face, I might be able to change her mind myself. How did the shop get robbed? What was up with that? There was no need to read Babywood's letter again because there wasn't any riddles or hidden messages. It was plain and simple, give me the word and I will knock Chance's ass off.

As I grabbed the third letter I read the address: Chance, 4450 Hotel Circle Drive. San Diego CA. 92106.

That was the address where Treasure and I lived. At first it didn't dawn on me, but after reading his letter it sure as hell did.

First and foremost, I want to say as a soldier I respect everything about you! Now, to the reason why I'm writin' you. Nu'voe, you and me always kept it real wit' each other while we we're doin' time, well at least you did. You reached out and asked me to handle somethin' for you and I agreed. That shit was stupid of you to do. It was stupid to put a nigga like me around a bitch like Treasure. To make a long story short, Treasure wit' me now and don't worry 'bout the ends you promised me. I've already been compensated. By the way, good luck wit' yo' trial. I tried homie!

Chance

P.S.

You ain't ever lied. The pussy fire like you always said it was. (SMH)

"Fuck nigga!" were the words that my mind transferred to my mouth.

This nigga Chance had stabbed me in the back. My thoughts started running wild.

"Don't worry 'bout the ends you promised me. I've already been compensated."

He was fucking my bitch and the nigga robbed me!

"Damn, Treasure. How could you?"

I had to get the hell up out of jail. "Nu'voe, you stupid than a mutha-fucka. How could you trust a nigga you met in jail? What you gonna do now? I gotta talk to Treasure. Nigga, get'cha shit right. The bitch wit' him now and for who knows how long. She's takin' the stand against you. You sucka fo' love ass nigga! Wake up, Nu'voe!" I was cursing myself out.

With Chance's letter it felt like I had been checkmated. I tossed his letter on top of my locker right along with the others, laid on my bunk, put my hands behind my head, and thought about the life I use to have.

"Nu'voe, what's up, homie?" a voice came booming through the vent.

It was my next door neighbor, Bullet. He was a Mexican from Los Angeles, and us both being from California we fucked with each other on a daily basis.

"What up, Bullet?" I shot back, still lying on my bunk.

"I saw you had that mail in yo' hands home's. Did that stripper bitch send them shots? I got some stamps I'm tryna spend, Nu'vaar."

"Nah Bullet not yet," I replied with no life in my words.

The letters I had just received damn near killed me.

"Fuck that bitch, home'z. What about that legal shit? What they talkin' 'bout?"

"Oh, shit!" I blurted out as I jumped off my bunk and grabbed the manila envelope I had picked up from my counselor.

It had slipped my mind. The fuck shit I received from the streets had me off balance. I anxiously opened the envelope and the first thing I saw was *UNITED STATES OF AMERICA VS. NU'VAAR DAVOE.*

"Nu'voe! Nu'voe! Nu'voe!" Bullet was still calling me through the vent.

"Not right now, Bullet. I'll get back to you later," I replied as I continued to read the papers inside the envelope.

The only real statement that meant anything to me was: United States of America VS. Nu'vaar Davoe. The courts have erred in plain view. We the United States drop all charges against one Nu'vaar Davoe 03755-298. We also push for an immediate release. My heart dropped, and I sat back down on my bunk as tears flowed from my eyes. They were tears of happiness and sorrow.

I was happy because I was going home, but I was sad because I was going home to address Treasure, Chance, and Trust. First, I needed to put a plan together.

CHAPTER TWENTY
LANISE

I got my ass up and cleaned the house. I had been kind of down and really missed my man. He had been in California for about a month or so for some bullshit. He came home for a day and went right back telling me he opened a business out there. I'm not tripping for real. He dropped me 15 G's, some good dick, and a kiss on the cheek. That Cali sun gave him a good tan, and my baby was looking good. I know them bitches are all over my man out there. I wasn't worried about it because I found out that I was pregnant. I didn't know if it was Chance's or his daddy's. I know it's some bullshit, but for his pops to be fifty-five years old, he knew how to touch every wall my pussy has.

My thoughts were interrupted by the sound of my doorbell.

"Who the fucks ringing my bell at this time of day? Probably the mail man."

I looked out the window and the face I saw caused me to do a double take.

"Nu'voe!" I smiled as I greeted him at the door. "Hey, what's going on?"

I smiled and hugged him a little longer than I was supposed to. *Damn, he's fine* I thought to myself as I watched his eyes roam all over my body.

"What's happenin', Lanise?" he smiled again. "You looking good," he said, while giving me another once over.

I was wearing a pair of Chance's boxers and a tank top with no bra. My ass filled up every thread of cotton and my nipples stood at full attention. My hair was pulled back into a ponytail, and I was looking cute with no make-up or nothing.

So, a few weeks prior Nu'voe wrote me saying he needed a place to stay. I thought it would be cool to surprise Chance. It also would be good to have a man in the house while Chance was in Cali doing God knows what. So I called his case manager and Voila, he was at my doorstep.

I sashayed to the couch. He sat across from me looking cute in his grey sweat suit and cheap looking Nikes.

"Gotta take him shopping, A.S.A.P," I mumbled to myself. I got up to put on some music. "So, I know you happy to be free." I said to him, making conversation.

"Ah man, you already know. Finally home and ready to put some plans in motion," he answered while staring at me and licking his lips like LL Cool J.

Did my pussy just do what I think it did? I thought to myself, feeling moistness between my thighs.

I smiled a devilish grin, and said, "So, I know you wanna get up out them clothes and go shopping. Chance got some new shit he's never worn for the time being. Let me get you some new underwear and all that so you can get comfortable and take you a hot shower."

I went to get him a bath towel and underwear before leading him to the bathroom. When we entered me and Chance's oversized bathroom he was in shock.

"This some real playa's shit right c'here," he said in his Cali accent, admiring the Maplewood double sink.

When I bent over to get the soap and lotion and also giving him an eye full, what happened next took me by surprise. He gripped me by my hair and pulled me to face him. At first fear overwhelmed me, but when he put his tongue down my throat it was on and popping.

I melted in his mouth and opened my legs wide, welcoming him inside of me. When he removed the boxers and put his lips on this pussy I damn near fainted. He sucked on my phat ass clit like his life depended on it. After I had enough, I pulled at his sweatpants to get that meat and boy was I impressed when I laid eyes on it. I hopped off the sink and dropped to my knees.

CHAPTER TWENTY-ONE
NU'VOE

The shit is crazy. I was standing in the bathroom of the nigga that crossed me with my dick seven inches deep in his bitch's throat. The bitch was working it like a pro. I was actually feeling fucked up about what I was doing and going to do. I've always tried to live my life by the no-no rules, and at that moment I was breaking one of the cardinal rules.

"Fuckin' around wit' one of yo' boy's bitches."

Fuck that shit! The nigga crossed the line when he decided to slip, fall, and put his dick in Treasure so it was no holds-barred. When you're a man in love you tend to do stupid shit!

FIFTEEN MINUTES LATER...

All cleaned up and fresh with some of this nigga Chance's gear on, his bitch and I was on the way to the mall. After she swallowed some of my future babies, I put a seven-minute smack down on her. It was only seven minutes, but it felt like 70. I hadn't had any good pussy in years because Ms. Burnes' fat ass didn't count.

The way Lanise's pussy muscles gripped my dick and that wet, warm silky feeling caused a nigga to cum way before I planned to.

After I beat the pussy up, she wanted to take me shopping and as we rode I could tell that something was bothering her. I asked her what is was and just like a bitch with problems on her chest she told me everything. After hearing her story, for some reason it made what I was about to do much easier. As a player, I did the unthinkable. I told Lanise that her man was sleeping with Treasure, my woman.

I told her the reason why Chance was in California was because he was cheating on her. I explained how I felt betrayed, and I put it on as thick as I could.

I could tell that Lanise was all but through with Chance's ass by the story she told me and by her letting me deposit my dick funds in her mouth bank. I thought what I had just told her would have changed her mind about shopping, but it did the total opposite. Lanise went into the mall and lost her mind. The bitch spent 10 G's on me and another five on herself. So much for the $15,000 Chance left her.

This is the type of bitch you would definitely regret leaving anything with because if she ever got mad at you, what you have will quickly become what you had.

The trip back from the mall was more interesting than the trip going. Feeling like she had been betrayed, Lanise told me a crazy story about how she and Chance's father stole Chance's money while he was locked up. The thing that made the conversation even crazier was the fact that she concocted a plan to have Chance's father set up for the rest of the money. It was supposed to be somewhere around a 100 G's and guess who was going to be the stick up man, yours truly.

Blinded by love, hate, disloyalty, and Lanise's lips wrapped tight around my dick I agreed. 100 G's was nice, but the thought of getting back at Chance caused my dick to grow two more inches. I grabbed Lanise by her ponytail and fucked the shit out of her mouth as we drove back to her spot.

CHAPTER TWENTY-TWO
DIAMOND

My dumb ass forgot to put my phone number in the letter and I fucked my phone up so I couldn't email him. I knew Nu'voe wanted to reach out to me. The letter didn't come back so I knew he had gotten it. I was lost in thought while I was in the shop doing this wanna be video vixen's hair.

"Diamond, you going to the Keisha Cole's party this weekend?" Bianca had the nerve to ask me.

We weren't even feeling each other like that. Ever since that Up North nigga got here, she and Treasure had been acting weird!

"I don't know, girl. Maybe," I said in my phoniest voice.

Chance started strolling in with his swagger turned all the way up. He was sexy, but my mind, heart, and pussy were somewhere else.

"Hey, Chance," Bianca said as she smiled like she had a teenage crush.

"Hey ladies, how's everybody doing today?" he asked as he smiled at all the customers.

I had to throw some kind of salt in the game.

"Umm, let me call Treasure and let her know you're here," I said to Chance, trying to get under his skin.

"That won't be necessary," he shot right back.

I called anyway. As soon as I dialed her number the phone in his hand went off.

He looked directly at me, and said, "She not here right now leave a message."

It made me so mad. Then he goes and whispers something in Bianca's ear that had her all cheesing and shit. Next thing you know, they disappeared in Treasure's office.

"I can't stand these ho ass bitches. Ahh!" I stopped doing the girl's hair and dialed 411. "Yes ma'am, Leavenworth, Kansas-The number to the federal prison. Yes, the USP."

"Hold please," the operator returned with the phone number to the prison. "Would you like to be connected?"

"Yes please," I said as I waited patiently.

I'll act like his mother with a family emergency.

A female's voice came through the phone, "Leavenworth USP, how may I direct your call?"

"Yeah, I would like to report a death in the family to my son, inmate Nu'vaar Duvoe," I said in a slight worried tone.

"Do you have his register number? Just to make the process easier, ma'am?"

"Yes I do. It's 03755-298."

"Hold please," the woman said. I waited a few seconds until she came back to the phone. "Ma'am, he's no longer here. He's been released."

My heart did a back flip.

"Excuse me! Did I hear you correctly? Did you say he's been released?"

"Yes ma'am, three days ago. That's all the information I'm allowed to give at this time."

"Okay, thank you, ma'am."

I hung up the phone, leaned back against the glass, and then took a deep breath. *I know Treasure doesn't know he's out*, I thought as I watched Bianca and Chance come out of the office with smiles on their faces. It was obvious what was going on in there because of the moans coming from the room that a few customers made comments on.

That's fucking crazy. She's fucking in our boss' office, I couldn't help but think. I wondered what Treasure's reaction was going to be when she found this shit out, but where the fuck was she?

CHAPTER TWENTY-THREE
TREASURE

"Listen, I'm just not feeling this anymore," I told Lil' Face. "I got a bad feeling about all this stuff that we're doing!" I yelled and then continued to yell at him for twenty minutes.

We had been going back and forth about the bullshit.

"What the fuck do you mean you not feeling this?" he yelled to the top of his lungs. "It was all good when I was hittin' you off wit' bread though, and suckin' ya stank ass pussy!"

I couldn't believe what I heard come out of his mouth. I was a lot of things but broke and stinky have never been my style. He had me fucked up!

"Your uncle wouldn't approve of this," I said, trying another angle, which in turn only made matters worse.

"My Uncle? Bitch, my uncle wouldn't approve of you runnin' around here with Chance neither now would he?"

That was unexpected and I didn't even know how to respond. I sat on the couch and cried. I had to tell him the truth or at least part of it. I couldn't keep holding it in.

"Lil' Face," I called out to get his attention.

"What!" he yelled as he sat down next to me on the couch.

I turned to face him, and said, "I have somethin' to tell you. It's bad. I-I really messed up." I stuttered, trying to gather my thoughts.

"What's wrong, Treasure? What are you talking about?" his tone softened a bit.

I had to lay it on real thick.

"The cops- they- been threatening me and I—"

"Tell me, Treasure. You can tell me anything," he said as he pulled the hairs off my face.

"Listen, the feds told me they were gonna charge me if I didn't testify," I cried, unable to hold it back.

"And what did you say?" he asked.

Before I gave him an answer I had to make sure he understood where I was coming from.

"Listen, you have to understand that I've been on my own all my life. I'm twenty-eight years old and I have never been in any trouble," I explained. "No matter what Nu'voe has done to me I never left his side. After all the cheating and bitches calling my phone, I have never crossed him. When he went to jail, I stood tall and held him down. I never knew that this whole time they weren't only watching him, but they were watching us. They have pictures of everything and everybody. They even showed me a picture of you but never mentioned ya name. I'm not built for this. I would have never signed my name on the house, cars, or the businesses if I'd known all this would come with it."

I tried my hardest to help him see my side of the story.

He backed away slightly.

"You still haven't told me what you said to them."

I decided to just come out with it, and said, "I agreed to testify."

Before the last piece of air escaped my lips he slapped me so hard.

Whack!

I never even saw that shit coming. He backhanded me out of my seat. I hit the floor and curled up in a fetal position, trying to block his punches.

"You fuckin' ratted!"

He then kicked me in my ribs.

"Please-Please-Stop-Wait-Wait!" I cried and pleaded for the beating to stop.

I saw my life flashing before my eyes. I saw my mom and dad fighting. I saw my favorite teddy bear. Everything. It all flashed before my eyes. When I gained the power to look up he had his gun aimed at my head. The lock in his eyes was of pure evil.

"Did Chance put you up to this? Huh? To get rid of my uncle!" he yelled.

"No, no! This has nothing to do with him I swear! They were gonna lock me up! Please believe me!"

He stood there for a minute then stormed out the door. Moments later, I heard tires spinning and that's when I finally had the courage to get up. I ran to the bathroom and stared at myself in the mirror.

"Look at my fuckin' face! Oh nigga you're gonna pay for this, bet that."

Luckily his punches hit my arms. That silly, young nigga didn't even know how to beat a bitch. My fucking ribs were so sore to the point that it hurt when I took a breath.

I cleaned myself up as well as I possibly could, ran my bath water with Epsom Salt, and then called my man.

I dialed my cell number from my landline and in two rings he picked up saying, "Hey, baby."

"Daddy, come home. You're not gonna believe this shit. Hurry up, please!" I yelled into the receiver.

"I'm on my way right now, baby" was all I heard before he hung up.

CHAPTER TWENTY-FOUR
NU'VOE

THREE DAYS LATER...

It was one in the morning and I was tripping like a motherfucker. This broad Lanise had me sitting outside Chance's father's house waiting for the signal to run up in there and jack his old ass. Before I went to jail I would have never been on any shit like this. However, between doing five years behind a big ass wall, the only woman I ever loved showing me the ultimate betrayal, and the fact that Lanise managed to pussy whip a nigga in only three days, it all had my mind in a crazy place.

"Grimey ass fuck!"

It was all starting to make sense to me, though. Chance was a scandalous ass nigga, and his bitch Lanise was even more scandalous. Those two were meant for each other.

The light in the bedroom flicked on and off three times. That was the signal. I took a deep breath and said a quick hood prayer. Ironically, I was asking God to protect me and keep me safe while I sinned.

I reached in the glove compartment and pulled out a pretty ass chromed Colt .45 with a beam on it. The bitch Lanise said it was hers, but I knew better than that. The shit had to belong to Chance. Not too many women that I know could handle a gun like that. Fuck a dog; this was man's best friend.

As I gripped the handle with my right hand, I pulled my SD fitted cap down low with my left, and at that point I knew there was no turning back. Ten seconds later, I was turning the knob to the front door. It was open just like she said it would be.

Damn, pops old ass was living right. He had all leather furniture, the biggest flat screen I had ever seen, marble floors in the kitchen, and as I walked through the living room my feet sank into the carpet. From the look and feel of things, pops had that three-inch super soft shit that molded to your feet. To top shit off, his old ass has got the nerve to have a big ass disco ball hanging from the ceiling.

After surveying the living room and kitchen, I pushed towards the bedroom where Lanise said she would be keeping pops busy. True to her word, she was doing just that.

From the corner of the door I could see Lanise in the reverse cowgirl position riding Chance's father like a bull at the rodeo. Right then, something inside me clicked and my mind flipped out as I thought about how this bitch was fucking that old ass nigga after I was just pounding her guts out less than two hours before that. The bitch had me fucked up.

Then I had to remind myself that she wasn't my bitch anyway. I was only there to handle business. All I could do was shake my head.

With my mind back where it was supposed to be, I pulled my shirt up over my face and got my jack on!

"Lay the fuck down and don't move old nigga!"

Lanise slid off the old nigga's dick and laid on the bed next to him. I couldn't believe that shit! Those motherfuckers were sexing on top of a 100 G's. What a hell of a fetish for pops to have, but too bad that fetish would cost him every dime of it tonight. I brandished my pistol and instructed pops to roll over on his stomach and lie face down. He looked like a fish out of water, trying to get on his stomach. That shit was so funny. It had a nigga weak from laughing so hard.

After pops was situated, I told Lanise to put all the money in a bag and to lie back down. I had to give it to her; she played her part to a tee. She got her Gabrielle Union on.

With the money in the duffle bag, I walked up to the bed and slapped Lanise on her ass then slid a 100-dollar bill in the crack of pops ass as I told him to tell his son, "Nu'voe said what's ha'tnin'."

When I turned to head out the room Lanise tripped the fuck out!

"Nigga yo' mutha'fuckin' ass aint leavin' here without me!"

When I looked back, this bitch had already put on her boy shorts and was attempting to put on her shirt.

"Bitch, you betta hurr'up!" I yelled back at her.

As I turned around I heard Chance's pops yelled, "Y'all got me fucked up!"

My mind told me to keep it pushing and get the hell up out of there, but my instincts told me to turn around. Looking over my shoulder, I saw Lanise running towards me and over her shoulder I saw pops reach up under his pillow and pull out a pistol.

"Fuck!"

Pop! Pop! Pop!

He fired in my direction and I fired back.

Bloc! Bloc! Bloc!

Five seconds later, Lanise and I were out of there with a 100 G's. It wasn't until we were on the freeway that I looked over and saw that Lanise had been shot two times. She was shot once in the arm and once through her back that was coming out through her chest. Every time she tried to talk, blood would ooze out her chest. She was dead as a doorknob by the time I reached her house.

The first thing I thought about was getting the fuck back to Cali. Before I could do that I had to wipe down everything I might have touched including the house and car. Then I made a phone call.

"What's up, baby?"

"This ain't yo' baby, nigga!" I said aggressively.

"Who the fuck is this?"

"The wrong nigga to fuck wit'!"

"Nu'voe? What the fuck! You callin' me from my—"

"Yeah Chance, I'm callin' you from yo' house. You got somethin' that belongs to me, and now I got somethin' that belongs to you. Make sure you holla' at yo' pops. I'm sure he has all the info you need. See you when I see you, bitch!"

CHAPTER TWENTY-FIVE
CHANCE

I couldn't believe that shit. I had to pull the car over and catch my breath after that one. Nu'voe just called me from my house, from my fucking house! How did he get out? Was this nigga snitching? He had to be. How the fuck did he get to my crib? My mind was moving at a thousand miles per minute. I had to get back to Jersey A.S.A.P.

There were tears in my eyes. The nigga had me crying. I haven't cried since my mother died. That shit right there meant war. I couldn't really be mad because I was fucking his Shorty who was set to testify against him soon.

Grabbing my phone, I called my crib over-and-over again and got no answer.

"Fuck!"

I thought about calling Justin to go over there for me before remembering that I killed that nigga a few weeks back.

"Fuck! A'ight I'ma call the homies from the set,"

I called my homie KG and he picked up on the first ring saying, "Yo."

"Ayo Blood, go to my crib A.S.A.P., and if wifey got a nigga over there rock-a-bye baby that nigga on Bloods!" I yelled into the phone, talking real reckless.

"A'ight, homie, I'm on it right now."

We hung up and I felt a little at ease. I hoped that she didn't let that nigga rock her to sleep. She better not have given that nigga no pussy.

Vrrr! Vrrr!

My phone vibrated on my leg, and it was KG.

"What's poppin'?" I asked when I answered the phone.

"Ayo, where you live, homie?" he asked confused.

"Ahh shit!" I totally forgot none of my niggas knew where I lived. "7136 Cliffside Drive, in Society Hill. My truck is parked in front of my spot."

"A'ight, I got it. I'll hit'chu when it's done."

He hung up. I had to go see what Treasure wanted that was so important. It sounded like she was in trouble. Either way, I'm heading back to Jersey today.

TEN MINUTES LATER...

As soon as I stepped foot in the crib she started telling me about Lil' Face.

"He hit me blah, blah, blah-He pulled a gun on me blah, blah, and blah-He's looking for you!"

That definitely caught my attention. A guy with a gun is looking for me.

"Treasure! Treasure!" I yelled to calm her down and stop her from saying so damn much. "Listen, Nu'voe is home and he just called me from my house in Jersey," I let the words sink in. "I'll be back in a few days. I gotta make sure shit is straight, and then I'll be right back. I promise."

"Uhh, you lyin' ass nigga. 'Vo can't be home." She went straight hoodrat on me. "He 'bout to get thirty years for all that shit I said about him. Mutha-fucka you just wanna go home to ya' ugly ass bitch and leave me, huh? I told you a nigga lookin' for you and you runnin' scared like a lil' bitch!"

Wham!

I smacked the shit out of her and before she realized what happened I pushed her against the wall and put both hands around her neck.

"Listen, don't you ever violate me like that! You hear me," I said through clenched teeth, spitting in her face. With every word, I tightened my grip. "Don't get it twisted. I was sent to kill you remember, but I fell in love with you. So don't make me fall outta love and stick to the original plan." I gripped just a tad bit tighter. "Now, I'm going to check on my house and home. I'll be back in three days. We are still together. I'm not leaving you, and I promise Nu'voe's nephew will pay for putting hands on you, okay?"

I let her fall to the ground, grabbed my shit, and rolled out.

****

When I pulled into the hotel parking garage, I couldn't help but think that I was being followed.

"This ma'fucker's home. Did he snitch on me about hiring me to kill the star witness on his case? Maybe Green Mile and Babywood wired up and caught what I did in the Vista on tape to get him out. This whole shit is a set up," I talked to myself as I let my mind run wild.

I hit the button for the elevator like 20 times, but it wasn't coming fast enough so I took the stairs. I took the steps two at a time, sweating like a runaway slave, which caused my vision to become jaded. The AC had to be off because by the time I reached my floor I was drenched in sweat.

As I made my way to my room, the mop closet swung open. As a natural reaction, I pulled out my pistol only to see the elderly housekeeper.

"Oh excuse me, ma'am," I said, while holding my gun to my side.

Once inside my room, I called the airlines. I had just missed an outgoing flight to Newark, NJ. The next flight wasn't until 7:20 p.m. and it was only 1:25 p.m. Having some time to burn, I ran some bath water and tried to clear my head.

"Why hasn't KG called me back yet?" I asked myself out loud, while looking at my phone.

I gave Bianca a call and demanded she be by my side at that very moment.

Like a loyal rider, she said, "I'll be there in twenty minutes."

I sat my head against the wall and analyzed what 'Vo actually said on the phone. My pops, my pops? What did my father have to do with this?

I had a very bad feeling about the whole situation, and at that very moment I made the decision.

"I'm gonna kill whoever stands in the way of me gettin' at 'Vo."

I just hoped Lanise was alright.

I heard the door open, and immediately I picked up my hammer and aimed at the bathroom door. I told Bianca to get the key from the front desk but still no one could be trusted.

Bianca opened the door and peeked in.

"Baby," she called out in a sexy voice.

To my surprise, when she entered the bathroom she was ass naked. She wasted no time getting in the bathtub and washing me down. We enjoyed each other's company until we decided to take it to the bedroom. Instead of drying off, we made love on the ledge of the window seal.

Those pretty, long legs laid perfectly on my shoulders as I slow stroked her for about 20 minutes. She felt as good as we kissed with passion. I had to look down and watch how she worked her hips on this dick. She met me, stroke-for-stroke. I came hard, and I came all inside of her. I carried her to the bed and planted soft kisses on her neck, lips, and face. I tasted all the way down to her navel and down to her shaved kitty. I licked her clit, causing her to rise up from the bed and feed me her main dish. Three nuts on my face and I was ready to fuck again. She bent over on all fours, laying her chest flat on the bed and making her ass part like the Red Sea. She stuck her hand between her legs and guided John Shotty into her asshole. Murda she wrote!

After leaving her asshole full of cream of wheat, I told her I needed her. I gave her part of the story and told her that Treasure was making sexual passes at me. I felt violated being Nu'voe's homie and her man. I told her that Treasure threatened me and told me if I didn't stop fucking with her that she would tell 'Vo that we fucked and she did.

"I'll do anything for you, baby," she assured me and her eyes spoke volumes of sincerity.

"A'ight, take me to the airport and drop off this rental. I'll be back in a week tops."

Vrrr! Vrrr!

I heard my phone vibrate from the bathroom.

"Oh shit, my phone," I ran to the bathroom. "Shit, five missed calls. Two from Treasure, Two from KG, and one unknown,"

Then it rung in my hand again. It was KG.

"Yo, tell me sum'in' good."

"Yo son, I'm out front of the crib and shit lookin' empty. All the doors are locked. Nothing seem outta place from what I can see," KG said with clarity and I let out a sigh of relief.

"A'ight, I'll be there shortly. Round up the homies. I'm on my way."

"Ayo, hold up, where Justin at?" KG asked. "Last we heard he was out there wit'chu."

Think fast; think fast, I thought to myself.

"He with these Hollywood white girls that got his nose wide open. I think he's fucking with that powder or smoking crack. I haven't seen him in a few days."

I had to say something to throw him off.

"Crack-What?" he laughed. "Whatever nigga. Ayo, hurry home."

After hanging up with KG, Bianca took me to the airport. After a quick dick suck and a goodbye kiss, I boarded my plane. My baby was full of tears as we parted ways. It took a lot out of me to leave her. Bianca was going to have my seeds, fuck that!

Jersey City, here I come.

CHAPTER TWENTY-SIX
LIL' FACE

She doesn't feel right! This bitch had the game and me fucked up. I don't know who the fuck the bitch thought I was. Not to mention, she had the balls to tell me that she was snitching on my uncle. Everybody and their mama knew that my uncle loved that bitch's period stained panties, but I still wouldn't hesitate to put her rat ass in the dirt. I wondered if Unk knew about the shit?

"Treasure? Treasure? Treasure? Why did you have to tell me some shit like that? Now what am I supposed to do? I know we were fuckin' and everythin', but I can't just turn the other cheek on some shit like this. Or can I?" The bitch had me fucked up to the point I was talking to myself. "Was the pussy that good? Lil' nigga you from the streets, where love don't live and all bitches are the same. They ain't shit!"

Fuck Treasure and fuck that nigga Chance! I wanted to holler at that nigga, and I knew exactly where I could find him.

As I pushed my candy green 2011 convertible Challenger, my mind did back flips, cartwheels, and Kung-Fu kicks. Treasure had just hit a nigga with back-to-back Hiroshima bombs, and I was driving around in circles trying to fight off the pain from the bitch telling me that she was cutting the pussy off. At the same time, I was debating on whether or not to kill this bitch for snitching on my uncle. By the time I'd noticed where I was, I was one block away from *Face 2 Face* Hair and Beauty Shop. As I pulled up to the shop and looked up at the sign, memories of my uncle flooded my mind.

This shop was named after me and my deceased father. His name was Big Face. When pops passed away due to a robbery gone wrong, my uncle opened up a hair and beauty shop and named it after us in my father's memory. Ever since I was able to understand that my uncle was, in fact, my uncle he'd taken care of me. He made sure that I had what I needed and nine times out of ten what I wanted.

Taking my eyes off the sign, I swallowed hard as I made a silent promise to my uncle and myself that whatever was wrong I was going to fix it before he got out of jail. That was my word.

The memory of why I was here popped back into my head, and I hit the green button on my keychain five times. That's when part of the driver's side floor slid open, revealing a secret compartment.

Inside was my baby; a .40 caliber gun transferred to fit a 32 round clip. This bitch was truly one of a kind. I put her in the small of my back, threw my hoodie on, and slid in the shop.

As usual the shop was jam packed with hood rats, ratinahs, chickenetas, goodie-two-shoes, baby mammas, wives, and widows. Being a man, when I stepped in the shop all eyes were on me. Plus, it was 90° degrees outside and I had on all black including a thick as hoodie. Who wouldn't stare at a nigga? It probably looked like I was coming up in there to lay the shop down.

I ignored the stares and one, two'ed to the receptionist desk where I spotted Diamond's black, pretty ass.

"Where that nigga Chance at?" I asked aggressively.

Startled, Diamond looked up at me. "Little Face? I ain't seen you in ages, boy. Looking all grown up and stuff—"

"Fuck the bullshit. Where that East Coast nigga at?" I barked again.

"First of all, this is a place of business. Secondly, why would I know where Chance is at? I'm not the one fuckin' him. You need to be asking Bianca or your girl Treasure where he is."

As soon as the words left her mouth she regretted saying them because I was on her ass.

"What? She is fuckin' Chance?" I yelled to the top of my lungs.

Diamond was at a loss for words, but the rest of the shop had plenty to say. Those hoes were chirping like birds in a coop.

"Little Face! I told you this is a place of business, and if you can't respect that you need to leave!" Diamond yelled.

I guess she called herself checking me. I let her get that off only for one reason; she looked sexy as hell yelling at me.

When she was done, I asked her could we go somewhere and talk. She agreed and led me to the office in the back of the shop where we most definitely got our talk on. As soon as we got back there I went in on her.

"Now, what the fuck was you talkin' 'bout?" I asked.

"Before we get into that, do you know that your uncle is out of jail?" Diamond asked.

"What?" I replied as I frowned up my face.

"You heard me. Your uncle Nu'voe is out of jail. Shit, he's been out for the past three days according to the woman that works at Leavenworth Penitentiary."

"My uncles out. Bitch quit playin' wit' me!" I yelled and balled up my fist.

"Hold the fuck up! You got one more time to call me a bitch, and my pretty black ass is gonna show you a bitch."

Diamond was going off on me again.

For a second there, I had lost track of our conversation because I was thinking about what position I could fuck her in. She was pretty, titties in a perfect C-cup, had attitude, and a 40-inch ass.

Diamond was bad. Too bad I was in a fucked up situation at the moment because I would have definitely tried my hand.

Finally, out of breath, Diamond stopped bitching and gave me a chance to talk.

"Rewind and tell me what the fuck is goin' on," I said.

I wasn't ready for what she told me.

"Alright you want it, well here it is. Yo' girl, Treasure, ain't shit! The police re-indicted your uncle and have been harassing Treasure to tell on him and she agreed. Today, I was wondering why your uncle hasn't written or called so I called up to the jail to check on him, and they told me that Nu'vaar Davoe had been released three days ago. If that's not enough, guess what I found."

"What?" I asked, anxious to hear the rest of her story.

"Treasure's diary, and guess what was written in it," Diamond said as she played with my patience.

"What?" I spat out, showing how agitated I was.

"Some of it you already know but the part that I'm sure is new to everybody is that Treasure's sleeping with Chance, and she's the one that gave him the code to the safe at the rim shop. Inside her diary she said that when she showed him around the shop, she had noticed that he was staring at her while she punched in the code to the safe. She didn't care because his presence around her had her pussy jumping and blah, blah, blah—"

This information had me hot as a firecracker, but I wanted to know what it was that I was supposed to already know about. I asked her, not really sure if I wanted to know.

"That you're fucking her too!" Diamond replied as she gave me a sly look.

That information rattled a nigga's brain for real. How the fuck did she know that? Nobody knew that shit but me and Treasure.

This stupid bitch has gone and wrote that shit in a diary. Where they do that at? I needed to get my hands on that diary!

"Where that diary at Diamond?" I asked with seriousness written all over my face.

"Where it's going to stay. Why?" Diamond replied just as serious.

"I need that diary, that's why."

I couldn't take the chance of my uncle getting his hands on it and reading that shit. I offered Diamond a deal I knew she wouldn't be able to refuse. I told her that I would give her five thousand dollars for it, and just like a money hungry ho I knew she was, she agreed.

We set up the time and place then I shook the shop. I didn't care what my uncle said that bitch Treasure needed to be dirted, and I was going to be the one to do it. I just couldn't let him know that it was me.

CHAPTER TWENTY-SEVEN
CHANCE

Urrrcchh! Urrrcchh!

The planes tires hit the ground and broke my sleep. I had drifted off, watching an episode of Sons of Anarchy on my phone. I glanced at the time on my phone and it read 9:30 p.m.

"Shit," I mumbled under my breath.

Then it dawned on me once again that the time in Cali was three hours back. Either way I was just happy to be home.

Quickly grabbing my bags, I hopped in a cab and headed to my house. My heart was racing as I envisioned catching Nu'voe in my crib. I psyched myself up by doing some shadow boxing in the back of the cab.

"Yeah nigga-Right jab-Uppercut-Right cross-Left overhand-Come to my house nigga-Right hook-Left jab-Fuck this nigga up-Yeah, it's on now."

This continued until I was looking at my house from the cab. I paid the man before stepping out. My house lights were completely off, but being from the hood I wasn't going out like that. I aimed my key at the QX56, got inside, pressed the brakes four times, and my secret box opened. This only worked when the car was off. I pulled out my Glock 9 then proceeded to enter the house. With the pistol in hand, I carefully stepped in. Everything was quiet. I flipped on the light switch. There were condom wrappers all over the floor.

"What the fuck?" I hissed as I made my way upstairs, following the trail of condoms.

I was furious after seeing all the blatant signs of disrespect to my household. I opened the door to the bedroom that Lanise and I shared and when I hit the lights I fell to my knees.

Lanise laid in our bed lifeless with her pants around her ankles and topless.

"Nooooo! Baby noooooo!" I yelled, unable to control my emotions.

I cried for Lanise. I cried for Justin. I cried for Nu'voe's family because only God knew what was in store for everyone that Nu'voe came in contact with. They were all going to feel it.

I quickly called 911, and then put my gun back in its compartment. The cops came and canvassed the crime scene. I spoke with Detective Tammie Porter. She questioned me about finding my wife's body. My plane ticket and receipts of travel ruled me out from being labeled a suspect. After a 45-minute cross check, they yellow-taped my house and officially labeled it a crime scene.

I grabbed all I could carry out of the house and when I jumped in my truck I noticed a sticky tab with my father's name and address on it. Nu'voe's words lingered in my head.

You got something that belongs to me, now I got something that belongs to you. Make sure you holla at ya' pops. I'm sure he has all the info you need. I replayed that conversation over-and-over again.

"What did he mean by that?"

Mentally and emotionally I was drained. I went to get a room at the nearby Radisson Suites. After a hot shower and a bag of that Cali I brought back with me I laid down and cried myself to sleep.

NO TRUSTPASSING

SIX DAYS LATER...

The following six days flew by. Lanise was set to be buried, and I made sure she went out in style. I reached out to Treasure but it was pointless. She didn't answer any of my calls. Bianca was my source of strength. She constantly checked on me and even offered to come out here to support me in my time of need but I declined. I wasn't going to violate neither Lanise nor her family like that. I talked to a few buyers about my house. I mean, I couldn't stand living in the same house my Shorty died in. I gave the Range Rover to her baby sister and parked my truck at a local garage in the hood. I used my Cutlass to get back and forth.

After the burial I met up with a few of the homies from the set. When I entered KG's apartment on Lexington and Bergen Avenues I met with L-God, Dejuan, Rajohn, and Nutty. These niggas were loyal and were about that action anytime or any place. KG was six foot one inch with a medium build, low cut, and brown skinned, and he was 28 years old. L-God was the shorter of the bunch and dark skinned. He was 30 years old and loved playing with knives. Dejuan was the wild one with long dreads and always bragging about his body count in the hood. He and Rajohn were brothers, both 260 solid but he was the opposite of his brother. Rajohn was quiet most of the time. Nutty's name spoke for itself. He was always doing some nut ass shit, and had been playing with guns since he was a youngin'.

After a walk down memory lane and four blunts later, I informed them that I already purchased their tickets and to be ready to leave in an hour.

"Ayo, don't forget to take the cab to Terminal C, Continental Airlines and wait for me there. I'll be there."

"Ayo, you want us to roll wit'chu?" KG asked, always having my back.

"Nah, I'm good. I gotta pay someone a visit."

CHAPTER TWENTY-EIGHT
DIAMOND

Looking at my Marc Blak diamond studded watch; I realized that I was meeting Lil' Face in an hour or so. This young nigga really had me fucked up, thinking that I was going to give him the real diary. Shit, I made copies then bought a diary that looked similar to hers and put my own handwriting in there. His dumb ass will never know. Plus, I have an insurance policy, my girl, Shavonne. I told her who I was meeting, where I was going, and if anything happened to me what to do. I didn't trust the nigga for real.

Finishing with my last customer, I prepared myself to get the hell out of there. Just as I turned around, Treasure came storming in like she was on something. The nerve of that bitch. She didn't even speak. I kept cleaning my station and couldn't care less about her nor her attitude. She'd watch her step if she knew what was good for her.

As Treasure was about to enter her office, Bianca was coming out and all hell broke loose.

All I heard was, "Bitch, stay the fuck out my office! Y'all bitches runnin' in and outta my shit. I run this mutha-fucka!" Treasure tore Bianca a new asshole.

Bianca snapped right back, and said, "Hold up you trifling ass bitch. Who the fuck you think you talking to like that, snitch!" I must say that was a low blow, and it was all over Treasure's face. Bianca continued, "Show me some mutha-fuckin' respect when you talk to me!"

Treasure wasn't backing down though, and she was pointing her finger in B's face.

"You a silly ass bitch! All y'all some silly bitches, and who you calling a snitch?"

I wasn't going to say anything but my pet peeve is when people say y'all instead of just addressing who they're talking too.

"Hold up a minute," I intervened. "Don't be saying y'all. You got an issue wit' B, then you take that up wit' B." I don't know where that came from but I kept going. "What, Chance got you acting all stank bitch?"

I taunted to make Bianca go but the look Treasure gave me was one of death.

"You don't know what the fuck you talking about Diamond! Watch ya' fuckin' mouth!" she barked at me.

"But I do," Bianca spoke before I could respond. "Yeah, Chance told me all about ya' triflin' ass, trying to fuck him when you know we are an official couple."

This boy Chance was good, too good. I had to say something.

"Umm, she didn't try, she did!" I had to make that clear, while also egging on the situation.

"You know what, fuck both y'all broke ass bitches!" Bianca screamed to the top of her lungs. "Treasure you ain't shit. You think you the shit, but you're far from it."

Bianca shoved Treasure back a few feet. I wanted to see a fight.

"You think Lil' Face ain't gonna tell Nu'voe he was fucking you? How you think that's gonna make him feel?" I asked while shaking my head, and throwing salt in the wound.

Treasure looked defeated as the tears streamed down her face. We all stood there staring at one another, stuck in our own problems and I'm so glad we didn't have any customers in the shop. This shit would have been all over San Diego.

Treasure dried her face with the back of her hand and back peddled out the store then jogged to her car. Once she pulled off Bianca and I stared at each other like two boxers fighting for the heavyweight belt. We were both heated and any flinch, jump, or sneeze would have resulted in blows right then and there.

Bianca fixed her hair back into a ponytail and adjusted her French Connection dress. She took a step closer.

"You stay the fuck outta my way. You crossed the line, Diamond," Bianca said, and then she let out a laugh. "You always wanted to be like me and Treasure, but you could never fit in with us. And for the record I never liked yo' ass," she said before leaving out the shop.

All I heard was her six inch Maud Frizon heels clicking against the marble floor as the tears fell from my face.

I felt like shit and that very moment I vowed to do whatever I needed to do to hurt them both. I should burn this fucking shop down. Yep, that's what I'm gonna do tomorrow night, I thought long and hard. Looking at my watch it was 8:30 p.m. I had to go meet with the little boy.

On my way to meet Lil' Face, I couldn't help but replay this week's events.

"Why hasn't Nu'voe contacted me?" I asked myself and couldn't help but to think back to the black eye that I noticed Treasure was trying hard to cover with all that makeup, not to mention the choke marks on her neck.

Trust me, I've had my ass kicked plenty of times before so I knew. Maybe 'Vo was kicking her ass because last I checked Chance was back in Jersey. Who knows, I thought about giving Lil' Face some head to get some information out of him.

CHAPTER TWENTY-NINE
CHANCE

I didn't have much time to do what needed to be done so I had to hurry up and move smoothly. Something didn't sit right on my heart. I had the address that was on the sticky pad traced and got a phone number. I've seen this number on my home phone bill over 50 times along with it locked in Lanise's cell phone.

Thanks to my big girl, Lashonda at the Verizon store, I was able to get all this intel.

It turns out all this time I had been asking Lanise about my pops, and she was in contact with him the whole time. One plus one is two depending on what you're smoking, and the bottom line is my pops had my money.

I left the engine of my Cutlass running as I approached the house. It was a cool little spot in Secaucus. A handicapped complex for the disabled.

I rung the bell and moments later his voice roared through the other end of the door, "Who is it?"

"Building security, there's been a disturbance in the area, can I come in?" I asked, hoping my fake voice worked.

There was the sound of locks clicking then the door opened. The look on his face confirmed that he was ducking me. He was stuck like a deer in headlights.

"Hey-Ch-Chance, you look good son," he stuttered, revealing bullshit in every word he spoke.

"May I come in?" I asked, playing off his fear.

"Sure-Yeah-Yeah, come on in, son."

Once I entered and stepped on his thick ass carpet and noticed his decked out living room set I already knew. I just wanted to hear him say it. I dug in, hoping he would take the bait.

"Why you do it, pops? Why you cross me for my bitch?" I paced back and forth. "What, you thought she wouldn't tell me?" I raised my voice and just like I thought the tears ran down his face.

He broke down.

"It was her plan. She told me about the money in the attic. I'm sorry son. I love you," he said with his head in his hands.

I just looked at him with hatred in my eyes.

"That's fucked up pops. How could you do this to me?"

He began to sob harder. "She had me robbed. Her and some nigga took it all and ran out," he explained in an attempt to regain my love.

"Was she alive when you last saw her?" I asked.

"Yeah, yeah she was alive. Her and some guy robbed me," he repeated.

He rambled on-and-on. I slipped behind him so I was out of his sight. He went on about Lanise taking the money and all this bullshit until I cut him off.

"She's dead, pop," I said from afar.

Hearing the news, he broke down even more and I allowed him to mourn. I pushed to the kitchen and grabbed the sharpest knife in the drawer. He cried so hard he never saw me coming.

"Son, I'm so sorry. You have to bel—"

I gripped him by the back of his neck and jammed the knife into his throat. Blood spilled everywhere as he gagged and choked on his own fluids. His eyes were locked on me when he took his final breath. I made my way back to the kitchen and turned on the stove to the highest temperature, and then I turned the central heat control to 90 degrees. I lit a cigarette, dropped it on the thick ass carpet, and then watched it catch fire. I looked at my pops one last time before I made my exit.

"I'm sorry, mother."

****

"Welcome to San Diego International Airport," the pilot said over the loudspeaker.

We landed, grabbed our bags, and were met by Bianca out front.

L-God spoke with lust in his eyes, "Damn homie, who is this?"

Bianca was looking good in her Michael Kors dress and the six-inch Alexander McQueen lace up, open-toed heels.

"This is my wifey, Bianca," I introduced her to everybody. "Bianca that's KG, L-God, Nutty, Rajohn, and Dejaun. Now that's out the way, let's get outta here."

Bianca gave them a runway smile before she spoke, "Hi, boys. I've heard so much about y'all and I have something special planned for y'all, trust me."

She winked, and then kissed me before strutting to the passenger side of the ten-passenger van she rented for us.

Nutty's crazy ass had the nerve to pull up on the side of me, and say, "Yo Blood, can we run that?"

He asked the question with a smile on his face.

I couldn't even get mad because I would have said the same thing. All I could do was laugh.

"Get ya silly ass in the van, nigga."

Moments later we pulled into the Marriot that was not too far from the airport. Bianca escorted us to Room 413 and when she opened the door there stood five, beautiful, model-type women awaiting our arrival.

Bianca led the way, and then she turned to face us.

"Y'all get comfortab e. Me and Chance have a conjoining room next door," she said before pulling me away to the next room.

My little niggas wasted no time getting it popping, and I knew they would be tied up for a minute. Bianca and I went two explosive rounds in the shower, and she filled me in on what she learned about Nu'voe. She explained how he had been showing his face around town and to be careful.

Vrrr! Vrrr!

Bianca's phone vibrated. When she looked at the text message she signaled for me to get dress.

Within twenty minutes, we drove out to an old rundown warehouse off the interstate. When I pulled in I noticed a dark blue, 96 Impala parked next to an old school, El Camino on deuces.

"Who is these niggas?" I asked her, a bit nervous.

"Trust me, we good. Follow me."

We both exited the van and the two guys hugged Bianca a little longer than I would have liked them too. They proceeded to shake my hand. The Spanish dude, who didn't say a word, motioned for me to follow him to the trunk of his car. When he popped the latch, what I saw made my dick hard. There were at least three dozen handguns, big and small with silencers. Then the black dude did the same but he had heavy artillery, Uzi's, Mack 10's, AK-47's, and pistol grip pumps.

I didn't know whose dick Bianca was sucking or what she was involved in, but at the moment I could care less. I was told by the black dude to take ten of what I wanted from each car, and then they gave me the bullets and extra clips for each weapon in a separate bag. That's what I'd call a sweet transaction. We made our way back to the hotel.

I put the van in park, and had to ask her, "So, who were them guys back there?"

She looked me dead in my eyes, and said, "Those were some of my Skyline homies. I told them that you and your crew was at war with the Vista niggas and they wanted to help as much as they could. This war been going on for years between the Vista and the Skylines."

With every word she spoke, I could tell there were hidden emotions behind them, but I let it go.

"I told you that I'm here and I'm ridin'. Fuck Treasure, Nu'voe, and whoever else gets in our way, baby."

Damn, she was getting into sexier-and-sexier talk and it was that gangster shit I liked to hear.

Bottom line was this, Nu'voe's ass was in trouble, and I hoped he was ready for this war he started. Killing my bitch was taking it to another level so it was on, nigga.

CHAPTER THIRTY
NU'VOE

It had been seven days since I had been out of jail and I already managed to commit robbery, possessing a firearm, witness of a shooting and not report it, possession of a 100 G's in drug money, and crossing state lines with it. Being fresh out, I broke every law possible. This shit could have caused me to spend the rest of my life back in prison. Shit, I needed to slow it down.

I got a 100 G's back to San Diego from Jersey the old school way. I hopped my happy ass on the Greyhound bus.

It took me three days but I got there. Wasn't nothing like San Diego weather, but 80 degrees damn near year round, not to mention home to some of the baddest women in the world.

When I got off the bus downtown, I was nervous as hell. It had been over four years since my feet had touched those streets and the 100 G's in my duffle bag just made matters worse. The first person I thought about calling was my nigga, Babywood, but instead I hopped in a cab, gave him an address, sat back, and enjoyed the ride.

When the cab finally stopped I was in front of my home. The house that I had bought for me and Treasure. The house that I remember sleeping in last. The house that Treasure and I used to make love in. The house that she disrespected me in and allowed another nigga to rest his head. I was sitting in front of the house where the only woman I loved besides my momma was in.

As bad as I wanted to get out and go inside, I just couldn't. My pride wouldn't let me. Before I confronted her, I needed to know some things. I wanted to know if she really was going to take the stand against me. Was she still in love with me? Most importantly, where was that nigga Chance?

Breaking out the trance I was in, I tapped on the Plexiglas window that separated the front seat from the back and told the cab driver to take me to the nearest hotel. Then fifteen minutes later, I was checking into the Radisson Suites near the airport.

The last time I'd been there was about seven or eight years ago. I had just gotten approval from my financial advisor, that I could open up my hair and beauty shop and Treasure and I celebrated with bottles of champagne and all night sexing. "Damn," I found myself thinking about her again. I swear to God she was like cancer. I was fine when I was not thinking about her, but as soon as the thoughts of her came, the pain was worse each time.

As I was checking into the hotel, I noticed a small group of niggas leaving the hotel through the side exit. If I had to guess, I would have sworn one of them cats was Chance. Was I tripping? I had to be. The long bus ride, sitting out front of my house had my mind seeing things that really weren't there. I shook off the trippyness, got situated in my room and put together my plan to get my woman, my house and my life back! The first person I called was my ace boom coom.

"Welcome to the player's line."

"Players line? Nigga, please."

"Who dis?"

"Nigga dis Nu'voe!"

"Where you at?"

I gave Babywood the address to where I was at and then I called my boy Butch.

"Butch Logan. What's ha'tnin'? You still eatin' them porkrinds?"

NO TRUSTPASSING

"Nu'voe, what it do baby?"

"I'm home. That's what it do?"

"Home? Quit bullshitin' 'Vo."

"Only thing bullshitin' 'bout me is my pat'nah on the phone. Check it out, Wood on his way already, so get down here a.s.a.p.!"

I slid Butch the address, hung up, and called Diamond. She didn't answer. I tried again but got the same results. After getting the voice mail again I said fuck it and decided to pull the money out of the duffle bag and count it until the homies showed up.

Babywood was the first to arrive. When I opened the door the look on his face was pure shock. The nigga hugged me like he thought he was never going to see me again. By the time Butch showed up I was halfway through counting the money and halfway through the crazy ass story about what had happened.

Butch's expression was very different than Babywood's when I opened the door. I had been around the homies a long time and could tell what they were thinking just by their facial expressions and body language. Butch's facial expression and body language said "How did this nigga get out of jail and how the fuck did he come up on this money so fast?"

Realizing his thought without him having to speak, I told the story again from the beginning. I told Wood and Butch to get the homies ready. I was sure once Chance found his girl dead and found out I had his money that he was going to be ready for war.

I had done five years in prison with this nigga. I knew he wasn't a punk and he was a beast with a shank. I could only imagine how he was on the streets with a gun.

"Why the fuck you sent this nigga out here anyway? You should have had us handle that shit." Babywood spoke as he brought me out of my day dream about Chance with a pistol.

127

"This some shit you suppose to have yo' real niggas handle. Not some nigga you met in jail." Butch added salt to my open wound following behind what Babywood had just said.

I don't know if I was tripping or not but I read deeper into what they had just said to me and what I got out of it was "Nu'voe you tellin' us that you don't trust us." Anybody in the game knows that once your boys feel like you don't trust them, betrayal is soon to follow. Right then I tried to sugar coat the situation, but in the back of my mind I knew that sometime in the future this might definitely be a problem.

I put the rest of my plan together and prayed to the man upstairs that I wouldn't witness any more disloyalty, disrespect, or TrustPassing. The homies left and I kicked my feet up, closed my eyes and once again let my mind ride that tidal wave. All I could think about was Treasure. Treasure. Treasure.

CHAPTER THIRTY-ONE
LIL' FACE

As I looked at my watch I noticed that the battery in my G-Shock had died on me so I pulled out my IPhone and checked the time. "Damn!" It was fifteen minutes passed the time I was supposed to meet bourgeois ass Diamond so I could get this diary she was supposed to have.

I still couldn't believe that Treasure was stupid enough to write that shit about us in a diary. I thought only young white girls from 90210 had diaries.

First, she let a young nigga like me hit even though she was supposed to be my uncle's bitch, then she decides to snitch on him, and then starts fucking wit' his homie from jail. To top it all off this dingy ass bitch wrote it all down in diary and left it where somebody could find it. The bitch was dumber than I thought. You supposed to take shit like that to your grave, not write down in a diary.

I rolled up some of that medical and fifteen minutes later I was parking my ride and sat there listening to Lil' Wayne's, Fuck You, single.

Once the song ended, I hopped out and pushed to where Diamond and I were supposed to meet. When I walked up, this bitch had her nose in the air and was talking big shit.

DIAMOND

I couldn't believe this nigga. For somebody that acted as if they really wanted something, he sure took his time getting here. He was 30 minutes late and had the nerve to act as if he was right on time. I wasn't tripping though, as long as he had that five grand. His trifling ass could have the diary. If he thought him having this diary was going to stop his uncle from finding out about him and Treasure, Lil' Face had another thing coming. I was going to tell Nu'voe my damn self. There was no way he wasn't going to find out that shit.

His young ass was driving a cheap ass car; he has no job, no house and was poorly dressed. His pants were hanging all the way off of his ass. I don't know what Treasure was thinking about when she opened up her legs for this little boy. She must have been smoking dope. That was like Amber Rose going from Kanye' West to Wiz Khalifa.

LIL' FACE

I let Diamond talk her shit for a minute but when she tried down talking me about fucking my uncle's girl, I let her know that she had me fucked up.

"Where's the diary?" I asked.

"Where's my money?" she shot back.

I reached in my pocket and pulled out five thousand dollars.

"Here it goes. Now where the diary at?" I asked again.

"Right here," she replied as she dug in her Louis Vuitton shoulder bag and came out with a Hello Kitty note pad.

Like two drug dealers making a drug deal, we exchanged money and product at the same time. She counted while I read. I was done reading before she was done countin' because all I needed to see was my name mentioned with fucking Treasure and I knew the product was real. I was about to leave when Diamond said something that stopped me in my tracks.

"Now that you got the diary, do you really think that your uncle still ain't gonna find out. Little Face, you're scandalous and can't be trusted. If it's the last thing I do, I'm going to make sure that he knows about this. I swear on my life!"

If the words she had said didn't convince me, the look she gave me sure as hell did.

My mind clicked into street code as it told me, this bitch was a witness to a crime and had to go.

Diamond must have read my mind, because she reached back in her purse and as she was bringing her hand back out I had already pulled out "Just in case", my little palm sized duece-duece and let off four shots.

Pop! Pop! Pop! Pop!

Two to her face and two to her chest.

The popping sound from my pistol sounded like fireworks going off and didn't draw any attention our way. As Diamond dropped to the ground, I rushed to her side to get my money back and to see what she was reaching for in her purse. When I saw what was in her hand, it fucked me up. It was a picture of me and my uncle at one of my Pop Warner football games. On the back of the picture, written in my uncle's handwriting, it said, "My nephew the son I never had."

My eyes immediately teared up. When I looked back down at Diamond she said, "He loves you like a son."

Those were her last words.

I got up and got the hell up out of there.

I had killed Diamond for no reason. The bitch had crossed the line saying she was going to tell my uncle. She had to go.

I had to get rid of the diary. When I finally pulled in the parking lot of the projects I put fire to a blunt to ease my nerves and fire to the diary to protect my relationship with my uncle.

What you don't know can't hurt you and it was no reason for Unk to know about this.

CHAPTER THIRTY-TWO
CHANCE

The homies and I hopped in the rental van, listening to Biggie Smalls while we rolled our Kush laced with Sherm. I was behind the wheel and Bianca rode shotgun. I caught a glimpse of her watching me from the corner of her eye. I had to give it to her she was the shit. She had told us that she knew where Nu'voe's mother lived. Being that he took someone I loved, it was only mandatory that he felt that same pain.

Eye for an eye.

"Yo Chance, you don't wanna get more rentals? I mean, in case we gotta break, it would be better if we ain't all in the same V, feel me?" Dejuan said, making a lot of sense.

FORTY-FIVE MINUTES LATER...

We pulled out the Avis rental car lot with four late model Dodge Chargers, all dark colors. Bianca led the convoy to 'Vo's mother's crib. It was 7:15p.m. Cali time and the mood was just right. The PCP was kicking in.

Bianca slowed down in front of this nice home that sat alone at the end of the block. She flicked her hazard lights on, that was the signal that we were at the right house. She sped off. I had to respect the fact that she didn't want to be around when it went down. She did enough by setting it up.

The weather was fairly decent unlike Jersey weather. I was really getting used to this type of scenery. I thought about even moving out there somewhere after I killed the nigga's whole family.

The neighborhood seemed quite so we screwed on our silencers. I exited the car and took my position while my homies spread out in case of any sudden surprises.

I knocked on the door while slipping my black leather Nike gloves on my hands. I put them behind my back. A woman in her early 50's opened the door and I immediately recognized her from the pictures.

"Hello, how may I help you, young man?" she asked while adjusting her bi-focal glasses.

I couldn't help but feel sorry for what I was about to do.

"Yes ma'am, I'm a friend of Nu'voe's. Umm, he sent me to check on you," I said trying to sound like a concerned friend of the family. She opened the door a little wider and that's when I gripped my hands around her neck so fast.

When I forced her into the apartment, my homies were right behind me.

"Check the house!" I yelled, to make sure she was alone.

Her eyes were bulging out of her head as she tried her hardest to free herself from my grip. Then I punched her in the face sending her flying through a glass coffee table. Pulling my ten millimeter I pressed it against her forehead.

"WH-What-What do you want?" she asked with tears running down her face and blood leaking from her mouth.

"The house is clear," I heard KG yell out.

I knelt down to be eye to eye with the old woman.

"Listen, I want to know where your son is right this second," I said between clenched teeth.

She continued to sob and cry.

"He's in jail. He's locked up!" she managed to scream. I brought the gun down on her forehead leaving a deep gash across her face, blood poured from the wound. "Ahh...Please stop!" she cried and pleaded for her life. I stood to my feet and aimed my gun at her.

"Your son raped and killed my wife," I paused allowing my words to sink in. "Now we're going to rape and kill you!"

"Take ya fucking pants off now!" I yelled to add to my theatrics. "I'm not playing with you, now I said!" I kicked her in the stomach and I watched her hurl over in pain and didn't feel no way about it.

See, when you beef with me, I beef with your whole fucking family. I looked over to my homies and was so high I didn't even realize the looks on their faces. The looks on their faces showed that they were taken aback by my actions.

I peered back at the old woman and saw she was inching out of her pants.

"Let me help you with that!" I yanked her pants off and ripped her blouse open exposing her fifty-year-old titties.

After I was satisfied with how exposed she was, I aimed my gun at her head and fired three silenced shots.

Pop! Pop! Pop!

I looked at my homies, and said, "I'm a lot of things, but a rapist I could never be. Now trash this ma'fucka!"

30 MINUTES LATER...

We were back in the ten-passenger van riding through the Vista projects. There were large crowds of hood rat bitches, and little badass kids running around everywhere. I'm determined to get this niggas attention one way or another. I rode through a little more and it looked as if they had some type of cookout coming to a close so I decided to see just how good this Uzi worked, I heard a lot of stories about them. I rolled down the driver side window and the passenger window did the same then the back doors flew open at the same time.

Everyone froze in their tracks when they saw us approaching. I yelled out, "EASTSIDE MA'FUCKER!"

Blat! Blat! Boc! Boc!

Multiple gunshots went off as I introduced myself to the Vista Projects once again.

CHAPTER THIRTY-THREE
TREASURE

It had been a long fucking day just sitting in the house sleeping and crying, crying and sleeping. It just seemed as though everything I loved I somehow manage to fuck it up or it would come back to hurt me.

My clock read 1:17 p.m. I decided to do something to unwind and relax. I ran some piping hot bath water and dropped a cup of Epson Salt, Seabreeze, and Victoria's Secrets Cucumber Melon fragrance in the water. I lit four candles, dimmed the lights in my bathroom, and proceeded to do something I hadn't done in a long time, smoked a blunt!

I laid my head back and allowed the hot water mixed with the green substance to take me to another place. With every pull I took, it seemed to push all the bullshit further and further away.

Halfway through the blunt I started to feel sexy and allowed my right hand to find my tenderness. I inserted my middle and index finger deep inside my pussy until I found my spot. I closed my eyes and envisioned the grimiest scene ever. I pictured myself on my knees and Nu'voe, Lil' Face, and Chance standing over me. I took turns sucking each one of their dicks until my jaws were sore and I loved all the attention I was getting. I could smell each of their scents and could taste each dick on my tongue.

I drove another finger deeper into my pussy as a chill ran through my spine. I was on all fours with a dick in my mouth, one in my pussy with another in my hand.

I was cummin. Chance fucked my throat while Nu'voe fucked my ass. My right leg shook uncontrollably as cum oozed out my pussy and into the bath water. I was broken out of my trance when I heard a bang at the door.

"Police! Open up!"

Police? What the fuck are they banging at my door for?

The banging continued until I got dressed and made my way down stairs. I was still moist. I wrapped myself in a Burberry terrycloth robe, and a pair of flip-flops.

"Coming!" I shouted as I approached the door and turned the knob. Opening the door, I stared at the two officers before me, and asked, "How may I help you?"

"May we come in please?" the female officer asked. She was a Spanish woman who was very attractive in her uniform. She had to be in her early thirties. Her partner was equally attractive. He had deep, dark chocolate skin, and a manly demeanor. He resembled Idris Elba but a tad bit taller.

"May I get y'all anything? Coffee or tea?" I asked trying to be nice and get to the reason they were at my house.

"No, ma'am thank you very much," the male officer paused and looked at his notes. "Umm, are you Ms. Treasure Simmons?"

"Yeah, that's me. May I ask what this is all about?" I became irritated. "We're gonna need you to come with us," the female officer said while checking out my apartment.

Not sure that I heard her correctly. "Come to the station? For what?" I looked at them like they were fucking crazy. "Am I in some type of trouble?"

"No ma'am we need you to identify someone."

45 MINUTES LATER...

I was sitting in the San Diego County Morgue shivering from the ill feeling of being in that place. The walls looked so slimy and the aroma reeked of death and pity. I became light headed and was ready to go.

"Ms. Simmons, right this way," the male officer finally rescued me from the hellhole. I got up to walk and my legs turned to jelly with every step I took. I was nervous, scared, lonely, and confused. I mumbled a prayer, hoping it wasn't Nu'voe under that sheet. The male cop put his arm around me, which I found quite comforting. The female cop showed no emotion as she pulled the sheet back. I lost my legs then everything went black.

When I came to I thought it was all a dream and that I was back in my bed where I belonged until I saw the handsome officer again, standing over me.

"Are you okay?" he asked.

"What happened to me? Where am I?" I asked.

He squeezed my hand before he spoke. "You're at the morgue. We just showed you the body of-" he paused. "The body of Ms. Diamond Davis."

Tears began to form in my eyes and I felt a lump in my throat. "What happened to her?" I asked feeling defeated.

"Well, we got a call that someone heard gunshots and by the time we arrived at the scene she was already dead. We found her pocketbook next to her with her business card in it, so we went to the establishment. That's where we learned that you owned the place. Also we found this." He spoke with genuine concern.

When I looked down and realized what he had in his hand I lost my breath. What the fuck was she doing with a picture of Nu'voe and Lil' Face, I thought to myself. "Umm, where did you say you found this at?" I had to ask again.

"It was in her hand at the scene of the crime."

****

I cried all the way back home. I couldn't believe that my friend was dead and I didn't get a chance to apologize to her after we had that fight in my shop. All I could do was shake my head at the thought that my girls and I were beefing over some niggas. Diamond was a sweetheart. Who would shoot her? She never harmed a soul. My mind raced as I tried to play detective. Who was she beefing with? Did she owe anybody money? What nigga was she fucking with? I knew none of the answers to any of the questions I asked myself. Some friend I was.

I had so much going on in my life that I had totally been ignoring my girl. That wasn't like me.

I drifted off to sleep and when I awoke it was 3:21a.m. I decided to call Bianca but got the answering machine. I left a message and let her know it was urgent to call me back. I needed some love. At times like this I knew who would always welcome me with open arms, Nu'voe's mother. I knew it was late but I called anyway. When I didn't get an answer I figured she was sleeping. I wanted to talk to her so bad. Nobody was better at listening than Ms. Johnson.

I could still remember the first time Nu'voe had taken me to meet his mother. Within the first 30 minutes she could tell that I was troubled by something and we talked for three hours. She was always a listening ear since then, especially when Nu'voe went to prison.

I tossed and turned all night with pains and cramps in my stomach. I couldn't shake the thought, why did she have that picture of Nu'voe and Lil' Face? Then it dawned on me. That picture was in my desk at work, how the fuck did she get that? Something wasn't adding up and I had to get to the bottom of this. I really needed to see 'Vo's mother to confirm if he was really out.

CHAPTER THIRTY-FOUR
NU'VOE

Babywood and Butch came to my hotel room to tell me that the plan I put together was in motion. The homies were just waiting for the call.

I had been gone almost five years and still had a big influence in the hood when it came to the homies. Feeling like I needed some air, Butch convinced me to head out and grab something to eat. We were just about to walk out the hotel room when Babywood yelled my name and said come check out the news.

All the shit I had been involved in, I wouldn't have been surprised if my face and name popped up on the screen. What popped up on the screen had me in disbelief and confusion. I felt nothing but shock, pain and anger. I was madder than the devil himself.

"That's mom's address 'Vo." Babywood spoke more to himself than me.

The news lady reported as they showed a picture of the house and a photo of my mother.

"Today, in the quiet community of Oak Park, the unimaginable happened. Ms. Diane Johnson, also known to many as Mom, a longtime resident of over 30 years was murdered in her home today. Report says that she was strangled and fatally shot. There is evidence of a struggle. So, she tried to fight off her attacker or attackers.

"Police also reported that there was nothing taken from the home, so it apparently was, not a robbery. Witnesses interviewed could not give any type of help to authorities. They all said that they heard shots fired and that three different colored Charger or

Camaro modeled cars sped off from the scene. If you have any information regarding this crime, please call Crime Stoppers at 1-800-ILL-TELL. Reporting live from Channel 7 news, this is Shirley Sherwood."

"What the fuck!" Babywood yelled as he looked down at his phone.

It was vibrating on his hip. I couldn't move I had just been paralyzed. The woman that had given me life had just been robbed of hers.

"When?" What the fuck! I'll be that way in a few." Butch was talking into his phone. His words broke my paralyzation.

"Who was that?" Babywood asked Butch.

"That was the homies. They said that some niggas came through and lit the projects up. Five people got hit. Two kids and three ladies."

"Ain't no homie get hit?"

"Nah."

"Who was it?"

"You already know. It was them east side niggas. They dumb ass yelled out eastside.

"'Vo, What's up?'' Babywood asked me.

He knew the life I lived before I came up on some money and changed my life style. He knew I was a rider, a killer. "Take me to mom's," I replied.

My mother had just been murdered in cold blood and the fucked up thing about it was that she didn't get to see her son before she died.

The ride to mom's was quiet. Butch, Babywood, and I were all thinking the same thing. "Eye for an eye, tooth for a tooth and Momma for a momma."

As bad as I wanted to see Treasure and get at Chance, my main focus was to find out what was going on with my mom and find out who had killed her.

CHAPTER THIRTY-FIVE
*LIL' FACE*TREASURE*NU'VOE*

LIL' FACE

I was sitting in the house where I was raised, fed, bathed, and whooped. My emotions were everywhere because I just found out that my great aunt was murdered and the police didn't know shit. Not only that, my hood was hit up by some cross-town niggas and these buster ass niggas didn't hit any homies.

Those drive-by asses hit kids and old ladies. I didn't even know niggas still did drive-bys, me and my homies walking up on you and letting that thing bark.

Who was shooting old ladies for nothin'? The way I was feeling, nobody was off limits. If you were in the way, you were getting hit. Plain and simple.

I wondered how Unk was going to take this shit. It was going to kill him.

NU'VOE

Nothing was clear to me anymore. My mind jumped from thought to thought and I saw nothing but red.

Butch kept talking about the projects getting shot up but my mother had been murdered so I didn't really give a fuck about the projects. Although I was from the Vista projects, I was disconnected from them while I was in prison. By him continuing to talk about it I was becoming irritated and had to keep myself from turning around and pushing his shit back.

Somebody had violated me, my family, and the street code. When you played this game there was supposed to be certain things that were off limits including kids and old people. I guess some people play the game by their own rules! They had pushed my hand. Whoever killed my mother had to die.

TREASURE

I was sitting outside Ms. Johnson's house. I came to talk to confide in her about all the scandalous events in my life and to ask for guidance, but I immediately saw that something bad had to have happened.

I took a deep breath and headed for the door. I had to see what was going on. I noticed that it was open when I reached the steps. I walked in and called out for Ms. Johnson.

"She's dead." I heard a voice to the right of me and when I looked in that direction, I saw Lil' Face staring at me. The last time I saw him he had slapped the shit out of me and pulled a gun on me. This time he looked so hurt, in pain, and gullible. He looked so vulnerable. I wanted to console him but knew it wasn't the right time or place.

"What happen?" I asked him.

The story he told me was hard to swallow. *How could this happen to this beautiful woman?* I thought. Nobody in this world is safe from evil.

Then I heard footsteps behind me.

NU'VOE

"Treasure?"

Her back was to me but I knew it was her. I would never forget what my baby looked like. She must have heard me walk in because she turned in my direction and our eyes locked.

Neither of us moved. We just stared at each other. It had been a long time, but my love for her had not changed and by the look in her eyes, neither had hers.

"Nu'voe!"

"Unk!"

Treasure and my nephew spoke at the same time. I couldn't respond with words. I just nodded my head. Treasure rushed to me and wrapped her arms around me so tight as she whispered in my ear over-and over, "I'm sorry."

No explanation was needed. We both knew what she was sorry for but at that moment I didn't care what she had done. I had my baby back in my arms and that was all that mattered.

When I glanced up at my nephew I could have sworn I saw him mean mugging Treasure and me but it was gone when we broke our embrace.

"C'mere boy," I spoke in his direction as I held my arms open.

"They got auntie, Unk! They got her," my nephew sobbed into my shoulder.

"Don't trip, you know we gonna handle that." I assured him.

An officer tapped me on my shoulder. "Excuse me sir. May I ask who you are?"

"I'm the victim's son."

For the next hour and a half, he questioned and filled me in on what was going on. He promised that he would be in contact with me. The officer left.

"That officer looks familiar," Treasure said into my ear.

NO TRUSTPASSING

Babywood and Butch came in and the five of us got caught up on what was going on. As we chatted I couldn't help but think back to where I might've known the man.

CHAPTER THIRTY-SIX
SHAVONNE

"I can't believe this. I can't believe she's really dead," I cried in memory of my girl Diamond until my eyes were red and puffy. I sat up in my bed looking around clueless with my mind stuck in a daze. "Who would do this to her?"

I kept replaying our last conversation.

"If anything happens to me, take this bag to this address," she told me.

I knew she was going to meet a guy named Lil' Face. I wasn't sure if I should go to the police or not. Damn Diamond what the hell was you involved in? I reached in my bottom drawer and pulled out the plastic bag she had given me. I wanted to check the contents but decided against it. The envelope she gave me with her signature read SHAVONNE, TAKE THIS TO 1265 OAKPARK LANE. ASK FOR A WOMAN NAMED MS. JOHNSON. LOVE YOU GIRL.

Eager to get to the bottom on this I quickly got dressed. I hopped my ass in my Mazda 626 and headed for a few miles down the road to Oakpark Lane.

****

When I pulled up to the address, there were people everywhere. I noticed candles being lit with teddy bears being placed on the sidewalk. *Another black man dead on the streets*, I thought.

I found somewhere to park and made my way to the house. When I opened the gate all eyes were on me. There were several people on the porch so I called out to get someone's attention.

"Excuse me, is Ms. Johnson here?"

Everyone stared at me and I was really starting to feel uncomfortable. Then this brown-skinned guy came towards me and by the look of his face he was crying.

"Excuse me, did you just ask for my mother?" he asked me.

"Is your mother Ms. Johnson?" I answered his question with a question.

His body language was not welcoming so I cut right to the chase. "My name is Shavonne, I'm Diamond's best friend."

Before I could get another word in I could tell he knew her. He must've been the mystery man Nu'voe she spoke about.

He cut me off, "Umm, excuse me. Shavonne right?" I nodded. "My family is grieving at the moment, I just lost my mother. Can you tell Diamond to please contact me?" he spoke with so much sincerity in his voice that it even brought tears to my eyes. "Are you ok?" he asked.

"Are you Nu'voe?" I wanted to clarify.

"Yeah, that's me," he confirmed.

"Uumm, they found Diamond dead yesterday. She was shot four times and before she died she asked me to give this to you if something happened to her. Well actually to your mother, but-." I handed him the plastic bag.

"Wait, wait, hold up!" he took a step back. "You said Diamond is dead? What? How did this happen?" he raised his voice. "She asked you to give this to my mom?" he asked with a look of confusion.

"I'm so sorry. I don't mean to intrude. I'm just gonna go. I'm so sorry for your lost." I tried to walk away as the tears fell from my face.

"Wait... Umm do you have a number or something? We need to talk," Nu'voe pleaded. "I need answers."

"Yeah I have one... Excuse me I'm just going through a lot right now," I reached in my pocket and retrieved my phone. "You know Diamond spoke very highly of you," I said as I dialed his number into my phone.

I handed him my business card with all my contact information on it and made my exit. I wiped my eyes with the back of my hand with hopes of him calling.

CHAPTER THIRTY-SEVEN
LIL' FACE

Babywood, Butch, and I left the house to put in some work. We didn't have time to really mourn the death of my aunt. All I cared about was getting my hands on some heat. I was ready. We stopped at a gas station to fill up the tank just in case we got into a high speed chase with the police after we accomplished our mission. If the police were on to us, we wanted to be able to drive to Mexico if we had to.

I was in the back seat in deep thought. I had a lot on my mind. I was happy that my uncle was home but it fucked me up seeing him with Treasure. I wondered if I would still be able to fuck her on the side.

Butch turned around and out of nowhere said "I'ma keep it a hunnit wit' you. Let that shit go! Your uncle's home, that shit is over." At first what he said didn't sink in. Then like water on a shirt my mind was soaked. Butch knew I was fucking with Treasure, but how?

"What you talkin' 'bout?" I asked him.

"You fuckin' Treasure lil' nigga."

His response fucked me up and instead of trying to sugar coat it I kept it one hundred with him.

"How the fuck you know that shit?" I asked.

"The same way Diamond found out. The diary nigga! I'm fuckin' her. All you got to do is slang some dick and you can find out anything from her." He boasted and smiled.

I wondered if Diamond had told him about us meeting up for her to sell me the diary. My next thought was that when he found

151

out that she dead he was going to know it was me that slumped her. All I could hope for was that he didn't try to run that shit by my uncle because I wasn't going to hesitate to slump him either if I had to.

Babywood returned to the car after pumping the gas. We proceeded to execute our plan. As we drove there was an eerie feeling that filled the car. Death was near. I had butterflies.

"There go some of them niggas right there." Butch had spotted a small crowd of niggas in front of a liquor store. We drove down the block, got out the car and doubled back towards the store on foot.

With pistols in hand there was no turning back.

"The second I see the white of these niggas' eyes, I'm lettin' them have it." Said Butch as we approached the storefront. He didn't even wait until we were up on niggas. He just let his shit bark.

"Bingo," he said as raised his Desert Eagle and fired.

Clack! Clack! Clack! Clack! Clack!

All hell broke loose. Niggas were dropping to the ground, running inside the store, and hopping in and behind cars.

Pop!

I even saw one nigga's head open up like a smashed watermelon.

Once we felt that enough work had been put in, we headed back to the car. Then I heard and felt bullets coming our way. Somebody had started busting in our direction. Then the unimaginable happened.

I was walking ahead of Babywood and Butch, so when I turned around to bust back at who was busting at us, I was facing the homies. I just raised my pistol and fired.

Boc! Boc! Boc! Boc! Boc! Boc! Boc!

I just put damn near ten hot ones in Butch. Babywood kept running to the car. He started the car. He looked like he was getting ready to leave me but I met him right at the passenger window. I hopped in, out of breath.

"What the fuck was that?" Babywood asked in a panicked voice.

Babywood pushed the Chrysler 300. He quickly hit a couple corners and got us the hell up out of the Eastside.

I could tell he was taken aback by what just happened. He had one hand on the wheel and the other on his Tech.

"Butch wasn't any good!" I justified my actions. "The homies said that they got paper work on that nigga. He was workin' wit' the feds," I responded.

I showed no emotion the whole time I talked.

CHAPTER THIRTY-EIGHT
NU'VOE

I couldn't believe the sun was coming up and I was still awake. The night before felt unreal. It still hadn't sunk in that moms was dead. My thoughts were on repeat. All I could think about was who the fuck did this and why would they do it.

I knew it wasn't because of something I did. I had been gone for the past five years. I thought that maybe it had to be something my nephew had been involved in. As soon as I saw him, I knew that he was full-fledged gang banging. The way he left with Babywood and Butch with no hesitation told me that nephew was use to putting in work.

I wanted to have a serious talk with Lil' Face. As I thought about he should have been in college somewhere and not in the hood banging I just stared at Treasure as she slept. She looked so beautiful and peaceful. She was my baby, my heart. After my nephew and the homies left, Treasure and I drove to my room. We didn't even have sex; we just enjoyed each other's presence. We just talked and held each other. She'd talk. I'd listen. I'd talk and she'd listen. It felt like old times.

Being in jail for that time taught me how to pay attention and appreciate the little things. That's exactly what I was doing. As bad as my dick wanted to feel Treasure's insides, my heart told me to hold her and enjoy the moment. Admiring the beauty in my baby as she slept, I bent down and pecked her on her lips. She must have been waiting on that, because she wrapped her arms around my neck and pulled me down on top of her.

"Take it baby," she whispered in my ear with her eyes still closed.

Her warm words broke me down. They took me to a place I knew I couldn't come back from. Her words weakened me. They sparked a fire inside of me that had been put out a long time ago.

"Please baby, take it. It's yours." She softly spoke again and bit her bottom lip, this time looking into my eyes.

"Damn." She knows I loved it when she did that. That was my breaking point, and from then on I was her sex slave. Whatever her body demanded, I obeyed. Whatever her body said I heard and whatever her body asked for, I provided. The peck I gave her turned into the language of tongues.

Her breath tasted so sweet and her scent smelled so familiar. I had been away from her for too long, so I wanted to take my time. Slowly I slid my tongue out of her mouth and down to her neck. I softly pecked and licked her neck before kissing my way back up to her earlobe. I nibbled a bit and she squirmed. Slowly, I made my way back down to her neck and to her chest.

With the help from her, I peeled off her shirt. Her titties were the same as the day I left. Pretty, perky and perfect. Wasting no time, I wrapped my lips around one of her nipples.

"Ahh," she moaned.

Before I went to jail, sounds like that when we made love used to turn me on and it was no different.

With my mouth still wrapped around her left nipple, I caressed the other one with my right hand. With my left hand, I traced that invisible line from her belly button to her passion zone. With one finger I penetrated her.

"Uuunnnhhh," she moaned again.

The second finger made her arch her back. In and out I worked my fingers. The feel of her pussy made my heart beat faster and pumped extra blood to my dick.

My fingers went in and out while I played with her clit. Side to side she moved on my hand.

Her body shook, and then she cried out my name, "Nu'voe."

As her body relaxed, I released her nipple. I took my fingers out of her and tasted her juices. She tasted just like I remembered. I kissed and licked around her pussy lips, and then in and out I penetrated her with my tongue. The way she tasted, I could have eaten her pussy for hours. Treasure had her hands glued to the back of my head and was fucking my face. I had to come up for air.

I wasn't up for two seconds when I heard her say, "Take it."

This time the soft whisper was replaced by a demanding tone. With no hesitation I slid in her.

"Fuck," she seductively moaned.

With both hands wrapped around my neck she slowly winded her hips, around and around while I went in and out. Within three minutes I came and my body shook like a California earthquake. My toes curled and I could have sworn my eyes crossed.

To my surprise my dick stayed up. She must have realized that too, because she pulled me out of her, rolled over, put her face in the pillow and tooted up her ass. I dove in that shit like a deep sea diver.

"Fuck me! Fuck me!" Treasure was talking nasty to me. "Whose pussy is this? Is it yours? Fuck it like it's yours!"

If I can remember right, Treasure never used to talk to me while I was fucking her and she always wanted me to take my time when I was hitting it from the back. For a second, I had lost my rhythm, but she made sure I gained it back. She reached back with both hands, grabbed both of my ass cheeks and threw her ass back against me.

Smack! Smack! Smack!

She was fucking me!

"Tell me when you're about to cum," she demanded.

"Okay, I'm about to cum," I struggled to respond.

Treasure turned around so fast and put me in her mouth that she made me dizzy. All I saw was her jaws denting in and out. My knees buckled and it felt like one of my ass cheeks had caved in. Just when I thought the show was over, Treasure blew me away. She laid on her back and started playing with herself.

"C'mere," she seductively mouthed. Weak at the knees, I obeyed. Standing right over her, she rubbed her clit faster and faster. She looked me in my eyes, and asked, "Are you ready?"

There was no way I was ready for another round, but I said yes anyway.

"Nu'voe, I love you!" Treasure screamed as she squirted all over my leg.

I was shocked as hell. Before I went to jail Treasure, had some good pussy but she was kind of a boring fuck. She wasn't doing any of that freaky shit! I loved Treasure, but I was no fool.

SOMEBODY HAD BEEN FUCKING MY BITCH!

CHAPTER THIRTY-NINE
BIANCA

I lay in my bed staring at the ceiling thinking about my man and how shit was going to be when all the bullshit was over with. It was 11:30a.m., time for me to get pretty. I took me a scolding hot shower, letting the hot water beat my back while I shaved my pussy hairs bald how my man likes it.

When I got out I sat on my bed ass naked while listening to the sound of Jahiem blaring through the speakers.

I turned on my flat screen once again seeing the murder of Nu'voe's mother as headline news.

"They act like she was the fucking mayor or sum'in'," I sucked my teeth.

I had a slight headache and staring at the empty bottle of Patron let me know exactly why I was feeling this way.

Vrrr! Vrrr!

My phone vibrated on my nightstand and the screen read: TREASURE. I was going to hit ignore and send her ass to my voice mail but I decided to answer it.

"Hello," I said cut and dry.

She went on for about ten minutes about how the cops and her identified Diamonds body at the morgue.

"Damn, Diamond's dead?" I was stuck in a daze for a second thinking about the last time we talked and the foul shit I said to her.

Treasure also went on about Nu'voe being home and how she finally had seen him.

"So where y'all staying at?" I asked rather quickly. I hoped she didn't pick up on my vibes but I had to find out where Nu'voe was laying his head. This was some personal shit.

"We'll be meeting up a little later. I'll call you so y'all can speak," Treasure said all loose at the tongue.

I ended the call and decided to smoke me one. I twisted a phat Backwood, lit that thing and sat back as I let my thoughts go.

15 YEARS EARLIER...

"Bianca, girl you gotta come to this party, all the football players gonna be there, it's gonna be off the hook!"

My girl Toya carried on-and-on about this upcoming party. We were both fourteen years old but she was super-hot in the ass.

"You know them Southeast bitches don't like us, we can't get caught down there and you know that," I pled my case. An hour later I was shaking my ass on some nigga. The party was popping, located on Solola Road, and I swear it was about 200° but I was enjoying myself.

The fruit drink I had tasted funny and my head was spinning but after I got loose I was just that, loose.

Toya crept up behind me and started telling me that the guy's house we were at wanted to chill afterwards. My inner voice told me to take ya ass home, but the spiked Henny punch told me, it's whatever.

When we got upstairs to the warm, cozy home it was real quiet. Two guys awaited us in the living room. The guy that was introduced to me was named Rich and his boy's name was Tyshawn. Rich lit a blunt and passed it to me. My lungs damn near burst out of my body and they all laughed at me. The next few pulls I was able to hold my composure and inhaled the substance.

It wasn't my first time smoking but something about that weed tasted funny and me being naïve, I kept pulling.

Minutes later my body was frozen. I was stuck and couldn't move. It felt like I had old lady glasses on because the floor looked so far away. I tried to talk but no words came out of my mouth. I was too weak and high. All of a sudden I felt my clothes being taken off of me and then pressure in my private part. I was being raped! Although I was on cloud nine I could see and hear slightly. Through half opened eyes, I watched several boys take turns having their way with me. I laid there stuck with my legs spread open as Toya laid beside me in the same predicament. We laid there being violated in front of one another and there was nothing we could do about it.

Someone yelled out, "Yo Nu'voe, ya mother's home!"

We were then picked up and laid down on a basement floor. Thank God a few girls left their jackets behind and woke us up when they noticed us.

When I made it home, my blood soaked panties let me know that my cherry had been busted. I lost my virginity to a rape. We later found out that we were smoking Primos, a mixture of weed, crack, and sherm. Nu'voe's house is where it all took place at. I smoked my first sherm stick, had been gang raped and my virginity was stolen.

My mother moved us to Pasadena shortly after that. It wasn't until I met Treasure through Diamond when I decided to move back to San Diego. When she would talk about this man of hers I would just listen, but I hadn't seen him in person or in any pictures.

Then one day she showed me a pick of Nu'voe and his cellie when she was trying to hook us up. My heart jumped out my chest! From that day forth, I played my part and promised myself I would get mine in the end. I knew I had to have Chance, but not only because of who he was and how he looked. It was the look in his eyes. I knew some way; somehow I was going to try to have him kill Nu'voe in the long run.

I know he fucked Treasure. As quiet as it's kept, I sucked on that pussy a few times. She had some good pussy. Treasure was my girl, but she fucked up when she decided to turn informant. That wasn't part of the plan. I didn't want him sitting in a cell; I wanted him in a graveyard for what he did to me.

I snapped out of my daze and got myself dressed. I decided to wear my Vera Wang mid-tummy cut shirt with a low cut top to show this cleavage off, a pair of skinny leg French Connection jeans, and some Giuseppe Zanotti lace up six-inch heels. I sprayed myself with some Vanilla Splash and headed to my man's hotel room.

CHAPTER FORTY
*NU'VOE*LIL' FACE*

NU'VOE

After blowing Treasure's back out and putting her to sleep I did my one, two and pushed down to the lobby of the hotel to grab something to eat. I needed to sort some things out. The girl that came to my mom's house talking about Diamond being dead had me tripping.

"Oh shit!" Baby gave me a package and said it was from Diamond.

I went out to the car where I left it. I had to see what the fuck it was.

When I got back in the hotel I opened the package. It was a diary. It was Treasure's diary. I knew I shouldn't have been reading it but my curiosity got the best of me. I sat for the next 30 minutes and read myself to a blood boiling mad. There I was doing time in a penitentiary for providing a better life for the woman I loved and her scandalous ass was out here fucking and sucking every Tom, Dick, and Harry. I was ready to hop in the rental and shake baby, but I changed my mind. Fuck that, this bitch owed me an explanation! My heart wasn't settling for anything else.

I slid back to the room. When I reached the door it sounded like Treasure was arguing with somebody.

LIL' FACE

I headed to my uncle's hotel so that I could fill him in on what went down the night before. When I got to the hotel, before heading to his room I put a pint of Hennessey to my lips and took half the bottle to the head.

As I knocked on the door I heard a familiar voice.

"Who is it?"

I knew Unk fucked Treasure.

Nigga quit trippin, that's his bitch. Nigga that's your bitch! The Hennessey, lack of sleep, and Treasure's sweet voice had my mind on one.

"It's me, Face," I replied as I took the Lil' off my name because it made me sound more like a man.

Hearing who it was she opened the door.

"Where's my uncle?" I asked aggressively as I looked around the room.

From the look and smell of things, fucking had been going on. This bitch's wig was tilted on her head.

"He must be down stairs or somethin'. He was gone when I woke up," she responded.

That was all I needed to hear. I went in on this bitch.

The last thing I remember saying to her was, "Did you tell him yet?"

That's when the door to the room swung open.

NU'VOE

I busted through the door once I recognized the voices.

"What is she supposed to tell me? "I asked.

Both of them looked like they had seen a ghost. When these two disloyal, scandalous mother-fuckers didn't answer my question, I answered it for them.

"What? Tell me that the woman I loved was out here in the streets fuckin' every opportunity she got? Or that my nephew was one of the niggas she was fuckin'? Not only that, but bitch you fuckin' Chance!"

My last comment must have touched a nerve in my nephew because he reached back and slapped the shit out Treasure. The shit took a turn for the worse.

Although Treasure had been running around pussy popping on me, she was still my love. In all the years of me being with her, I had never put my hands on her like that. Seeing my nephew introduce his goon hand to the side of her face activated my protective side. In an instant, I was on nephew's ass. The look on his face was pure shock because I had my hands wrapped around his throat.

"What the fuck wrong wit'chu!" I asked as I released one of my hands and gave him a taste of his own medicine.

Smack!

He surprised the hell out of me when he returned my smack with a two-piece and put me on my two back pockets.

If I didn't know it before, I knew it then. My nephew wasn't twelve years old anymore. I had been in a few scrimmages while I was in the penitentiary and never had been caught like that. I had to admit, the little nigga had hands on him. There was no way I was going to let my own nephew slap my bitch and whoop my ass. I got back on my feet and I rushed him. Using my weight, I pinned him up against the wall and commenced to whooping his narrow ass!

My only mistake was that I took a break from whooping his ass to talk shit and let him know that I was still his uncle. I let him know that I was still Nu'voe from the projects. Next thing I knew, I was looking down the barrel of a .45 revolver.

Fuck!

My own nephew had drawn down on me. Things sure had changed while I was gone. With death staring me in my eyes, I tried to talk the gun out of his hand while he let me know that he wasn't a little kid anymore. The more he talked, the madder he got, and the more his eyes showed his intentions. I was raised in the streets and right then, I knew my nephew was going to shoot me. He cocked the gun back and looked me in the eyes.

Boom!

CHAPTER FORTY-ONE
*CHANCE*THE HOMIE*

Chance

Slurp! Mmm! Slurp! Mmm!
Bianca sucked and moaned on my dick like she had to pay her rent. Staring me in my eyes, spitting on my dick, then sucking it back up was the fastest way to get a new pair of shoes for real. She ran her tongue down the sides while holding my balls with her left hand and stroking me with her right. It felt like I was in heaven.

I'm da baddest bitch, lavish bitch! The ringtone from Bianca's phone sounded off.

She ignored the call until whomever it was called back three more times. She was so engulfed in the moment that it killed her to stop. Grabbing her phone, she flopped back down between my legs. She clicked the call to speakerphone.

"Hello," she managed to say before putting my dick back in her mouth.

A man's voice came through the speaker, "Yo B, shit got crazy on the Ave's today niggas came through squeezing and hit three of the homies!"

Slurp!
"Uumm-Who—"
Slurp!
"Uumm-Got hit?" She multitasked.

"Victor, Lil' Scotty, and Peanut," the caller paused, "but check this shit out, a nigga hit one of his own partners before they rolled out. The nigga Butchy from Lincoln."

That caught my attention when I heard, Butchy from Lincoln, I knew that was VO's homie. All this shit was coming together like butt cheeks.

"Ask him is he still living," I whispered.

She was so into sucking my dick, she could care less, who lived or died.

Slurp!

"Unman-Is he-He still breathing?" she managed to say with a mouthful, twisting her head from side-to-side.

She was sucking the life out of me.

"Yeah that nigga still alive. He down the hall from Lil' Scotty."

I stuttered trying to tell her to ask what hospital and floor they were on as my nut exploded in her mouth.

Getting the idea, the nigga on the phone answered my question, "Lakeside, Room 619."

After getting some of the best sex I ever had, Bianca and I went to the homies' room and laid my plan down. Some of them looked shocked while others were already down to ride.

THE HOMIE

The nigga was on some straight asshole, I want to go to jail type shit. Killing a nigga in the hospital?

Hell-to-the-nah! Chance was going too far with the beef shit. I checked my gun and made my way to the bathroom when my phone went off. I saw it was Vanessa. She was my old head who I hit off with a little coke here and there. She had some fire ass head.

"Hello," I answered.

"Hey baby, you still in Cali?" she asked with worry in her voice.

"Yeah ma, what's up?"

"Is my nephew with you? Justin still hasn't come home. This bail bonds man wants his money and his P.O. issued a warrant for him. Last I heard he was out there!"

I contemplated my next move. Justin was my little nigga. I was like a big brother to him.

I wanted to tell the other homies but they were so far up Chance's ass that I knew they would snitch on me. Chance was my nigga but I also knew he was grimey as shit.

I decided to make some calls the next day and place a missing person's report. I just hoped that Chance didn't get the little nigga killed. Or even worse, pull the trigger himself. Something didn't feel right.

CHANCE

We were outside of Lakeside hospital. Only one thing was on my mind: cutting Butches life short! I hoped he was conscious because I really wanted him to see it coming.

I found a parking spot for the van near the door opposite the camera. Bianca parked one of the Chargers closer to the lobby. The plan was in motion. Being that he was in intensive care we had to cause a diversion. The plan was to handle this nigga unseen and unnoticed.

When I reached the sixth floor by stairs a small crowd formed around the two elevator doors. Rajohn and Nutty jammed the elevators. Bianca was arguing with the lady at the front desk. She was calling the nurse all types of stupid bitches when I slid right by.

NO TRUSTPASSING

Quickly I found Room 619 and when I opened the door my prayers were answered. He was alone. I looked back at KG as he closed the door, standing point outside. He was heavily sedated. To make sure, I slapped the shit out of him five times and he didn't budge.

Fuck it! I thought as I pulled the eight inch Rambo knife and stuck it into his neck. I held his head to the side so I can hit the jugular vein. I pulled it out and stabbed him once more in the heart.

On cue, the fire alarm blared throughout the hospital. I wiped the blood on his gown and disappeared like a thief in the night.

When I got back to the van everyone was in position. I casually drove off like nothing ever happened. I stopped at the nearest gas station and changed the license plates on the van. Immediately, I drove to the rental place and dropped it off. I turned in the keys and rented two separate Dodge Voyager caravans. Once we made it back to the room Bianca and her girls were there waiting.

After a mind blowing nut, I sat in deep thought. Okay, got his moms out the way, got Butchy out the way. Now I need Treasure, Nu'voe, and that ugly ass Babywood. Then I could go about my business.

Then it hit me. I ran to the homies' room and called them to the balcony so we could speak in private.

"Check it out. After this, we going back home. I know y'all niggas been putting in hella work and I love y'all for that. One more mission."

I sat quiet reading everyone's faces before KG spoke up.

"I'm wit'chu. What's up?" KG stood tall like a real nigga should.

"A'ight check it, I got a plan to rid all this shit. We just knocked down two major figures in this niggas camp. So y'all can choose this one. We hit his mother's or his man's funeral. Y'all figure it out and let me know." I left them with that before exiting the room. When I got back to my spot Bianca was there waiting.

"You hungry daddy? I know this nice spot that just opened up, you tryna go?"

"Come on," I was ready to go. I was so hungry my ribs were touching.

We decided to drive Bianca's Nissan Maxima to get something to eat. I laid back and sparked a blunt while she drove through the San Diego streets. I cracked the sunroof and bopped my head to the sounds of a local artist from my city named Hood. Coincidentally, the title of the song was named, Fuck Friends, and I couldn't help but zone out and sing along.

Friends fuck friends I don't need'em/ Smile in my face but fa'real I don't see'em/Bitch ass nigga think he built for the frontline/ then run for cover when the guns out CRUNCHTIME.

That was exactly how I felt at that very moment. This nigga did my wifey dirty. I was on his turf, a long way from home, willing to die for my respect.

I couldn't lie, I fucked wit' Nu'voe. We were tight in the pen and I picked up a lot of game from him about that pimping. I just fell for his bitch and for that, she had to pay with her life the same way Lanise did.

Looking out the window, I noticed just how beautiful San Diego looked. The air smelled fresh and I really didn't mind the thought of settling down with Bianca when it was all done. And I loved the fact that my niggas were out in Cali holding me down putting in twerk. I don't know where I would've been if it wasn't for them.

****

Once she pulled into the parking lot of the soul food and seafood spot named Lucy's my stomach started doing flips. I put one in the head of my .40 cal and to my surprise Bianca pulled a

170

.380 from her glove compartment. I was in love and that sealed the deal for me.

We walked hand and hand into the establishment and awaited our seats. I requested a window seat just so I could see what's coming and going.

We were seated and she ordered shrimp scampi, a baked potato, a well-done T-Bone porter steak, and a long island ice-t. I ordered shrimp Alfredo and a Caesar's salad with a side of corn bread and Patron on ice. The service was cool and the food was tasty. We shared small talk and enjoyed our meal together.

I noticed Bianca had made a face when she looked up from her plate. I turned to see what she was looking at and then all hell broke loose.

CHAPTER FORTY-TWO
*TREASURE*NU'VOE*

TREASURE

Oh my God! So much shit was happening at one time. My spot had been blown. Nu'voe knew all of my disloyal acts.

The niggas were in the hotel room fighting and trying to kill one another. I was flattered and turned on by seeing two men going at it over me. It was confirmation that I had Nu'voe back wrapped around my manicured finger.

Lil' Face pulled a gun. Wait-Wait-Wait. I can't let this go down like this. I reached in the drawer where I had seen Nu'voe put his pistol. The sight of it scared the fuck out of me.

From the look in Lil' Face's eyes I could tell he was ready to kill his uncle.

With my finger wrapped around the trigger, I whispered, "I'm sorry," and then squeezed.

Boom!

NU'VOE

Everything around me froze. My nephew and I stood there holding each other's stare before he fell onto the floor holding his left side as blood poured from his midsection.

"Aww-Shit-No-No!" I kept saying as I knelt down trying to console him.

I looked up and noticed Treasure standing in the corner crying with the smoking gun in her hand.

"He-He-Was gonna shoot you," she stuttered, choking up on her own tears.

"Unk," Lil' Face whispered as his life was escaping his body. "Don't let-Me-Me die."

Lil' Face tried to breathe as blood gushed from his mouth.

"I'ma call the police," Treasure said in panic.

I stopped her before she could reach the phone. "No, go get the car and pull up as close as you can to the door. Pull on the curb if you have to. Go, now!"

Somehow I managed to get Lil' Face to the car as he must have lost a hundred gallons of blood.

Once I got him settled in the back seat I looked at Treasure, and said, "Go pull off!"

She raced to the nearest hospital. "Hold on Neph, hold on." I rocked him back and forth. "Run all the red lights, just get there!"

This was some bullshit. I found out all this crazy shit and then this happened. Was he really going to pull that trigger on me? He had been crossing me the whole time right under my nose and then he was screaming for me not to let him die. I couldn't believe it.

"Why Neph? All da bitches in the hood and you chose my bitch," I whispered in his ear but there was no response. His grip on my arm became frail, his body went limp, and his eyes were somewhere else. At that very moment I accepted the fact that my nephew was dead.

"The hospital is right here, baby. Just a few blocks up. How is he doing?" Treasure asked, still hi-speeding through the city streets. My quietness caused her to look back. "Oh my God, no!" she banged the steering wheel.

Was she crying because I lost my nephew? Or was she crying because she had lost a lover?

Reality kicked in. I was fresh out of Federal Prison. I had lost my mother and my hood got shot up. On top of that Butchy and Diamond got stamped. Too much death was around me, which meant one thing, too many police!

"Stop right here," I told Treasure.

She pulled over to a secluded area just feet away from the emergency room.

"What you doing baby?" she asked as I began lifting my nephew out the car. I didn't answer her. I just pulled him out of the car and laid him on the ground. I closed his eyes and hopped in the front seat. "Pull off!"

With nothing else to be said I left my only nephew, my last piece of bloodline on the sidewalk dead.

TREASURE

Are we really leaving him like that? What I have done, I thought as I drove back towards the room. The tension in the car was so thick. Neither one of us said a word. I was too scared to even look at him and I could only imagine what he was thinking about at that very moment. Damn, I fucked up.

When we got back to the room we immediately started cleaning everything off that we'd touched. We both stripped out of our clothes and put them into a garbage bag. Nu'voe made me look for the shell casing which I found under the bed. I watched him pour Pine Sol in the carpet and dab it with bleach. Thank God the carpet was dark brown so it blended in perfectly.

"Let's go," he demanded and I followed suit.

He jumped in the driver seat and booked it out of there before any fuss was raised or cops were called about the gunshot.

He stopped at the Shell gas station and quickly came out with a bag of supplies. He still hadn't said a word to me and it was beginning to scare me.

After twenty minutes of driving, he pulled into the industrial loading area where all the truckers parked their trucks. My heart began to thump as I clutched the door handle preparing to run if need be. It was completely too dark out there for the bullshit and I wasn't going out like that He reached in the back seat and grabbed the supplies along with the bag of bloody clothes before making his exit.

I couldn't tell what he was doing until I saw the bag catch on fire. He was burning the evidence that could link the both of us to the murder of his nephew, my secret lover.

Nu'voe

I had to think fast. All the C.S.I. and First 48 I watched all them years in prison had paid off. I learned that fire and bleach were DNA's worst nightmare. I just hoped my skin wasn't under his fingernails.

I couldn't believe he was gone and this bitch was the reason. She crossed me. She opened her legs and let him fuck. So she was the reason he was dead. I had to blame someone for what happened.

I walked back to the car and looked Treasure dead in her eyes. "You know all I ever did was loved you and provide for you right? You crossed me in three major ways Treasure." I let my words sink in before I spoke again. "You agreed to snitch, you fucked my flesh and blood, and you were fucking Chance when you knew he was my nigga. Look over there at that fire, look at it!" I raised my voice as I pointed at the flames. "That's what the fuck I feel inside."

This bitch had the nerve to grab my arm and say, "You sent someone to kill me, Nu'voe. What about that?" she said through her tears.

"And you tried to get me life in prison," I paused and watched her facial expression change. "I guess neither of our plans worked huh?" I added my sarcasm.

Sitting there watching her cry, I wondered if she cried when she signed that 30-page statement on me. I gripped her by her face.

"I love you Treasure, but I can't trust you. Damn, why? What you did was wrong and ain't no getting around that."

She cried harder and it was really hitting my soft spot. "After I find out who did this to my mother I'ma have to lay low for a while. I'm sure you understand that right?"

Out of nowhere she kissed me. Before I could protest the bitch had my dick buried in her throat. In a record time I released in her mouth and she swallowed the whole load and kept going to get it back up.

TREASURE

I had to go in for the kill and make my move. Fuck all that other shit I wasn't about to lose my man like this. I knew in due time he would forgive me and we could move anywhere in the U.S.

I looked over at him as he slouched in his seat with lust and passion in his eyes. We swapped seats and I decided to drive to this new spot called Lucy's. The easiest way to a man's heart was through his dick and his stomach and more dick. In the words of my girl Trixie from Playa's Club: Use what you got to get what you want.

We parked and exited the car and to my surprise he held my hand. I felt whole again.

The events of the day had my mind in a whirlwind. I envisioned Lil' Face's body laid on the street like a city bum and it hurt me to my core. To make matters worse when we were being led to our seats I locked eyes with Bianca. It wasn't the fact that I see her but it was that shiny ass baldhead that I could pick out any crowd as much as it was between my legs. As he turned around I knew all hell was about to break loose. It was Chance.

CHAPTER FORTY-THREE
OFFICERS CHANCE* BIANCA* NU'VOE* TREASURE*

CHANCE

My luck couldn't have been any better. The pussy whipped nigga had come straight to me. Even though there were about a hundred witnesses in the restaurant, there was no way I was giving him a pass and letting him walk up out of here alive!

NU'VOE

Treasure stopped dead in her tracks like something was wrong. I turned my head in the direction she was looking. It was just my luck, but as I reached toward my hip I knew I was slipping because I had left my burner in the car.

"Fuck!"

I wanted to rush that nigga and give him a real west coast ass whooping. He needed to learn about respect and loyalty.

The only thing that stopped me was the bulge that I noticed in Chance's pocket when he stood up. I swallowed my pride and got the hell up outta there.

BIANCA

Ain't this about a bitch! Nu'voe and Treasure had walked into Lucy's. I'm strapped, my baby's strapped and it was supposed to be on onsite. It was too many people in there to get it popping. My mind calculated our chances to get away and they weren't good. So I reached across the table, put my hand on top of Chance's, looked him in his eyes and said, "Not right here and not right now."

OFFICERS

It was a boring quiet night. My partner and I decided to grab something to eat at Lucy's. As we pulled into the parking lot of the soul food spot, I could smell the Bar-B-Q mixed with seafood before I even got out of the car. It was intoxicating; it had my hungry stomach doing back flips.

All of a sudden, two people came darting out of the restaurant and right in front of my unmarked car. I was forced to slam on the brakes to avoid hitting them. It was a good thing that I saw them because, they sure didn't see me.

"Aye, that's that girl we went to see about the one girl that was murdered at the beach." My partner said. He was thinking out loud as I focused in on the girl.

"It sure is."

Nobody could forget that face and that body. The guy she was with sure did look like he was in a hurry. I found a parking spot and my partner and I got out.

CHANCE

The coward ass nigga just turned and tucked his tail. The bitch-nigga didn't even say a word to me. The nigga might be goin' to get a piece. My mind talked to me as I watched the door to the restaurant close.

At first I was going to let him make it, but the gangster in me wasn't going for it. I hopped up and followed trail with Bianca right behind me. She must have read my mind because once we were outside she headed straight for the car. I quickly scanned the parking lot. I must say my gangsterism was on point. The nigga was getting out of his car with a pistol in his hand.

I wasted no time.

Boc! Boc! Boc!

He fired back!

Boc! Boc! Boc!

NU'VOE

Treasure was about to pull off until I saw Chance come running out the door with a burner in his hand. I couldn't just let the nigga run up on me and let me have it in the car. I hopped out with my shit and gave him what he was looking for.

He was with the gun play, but so was I. Both of us let off shots. We weren't hitting a damn thang.

"Freeze! San Diego police!"

When I looked in that direction, I saw a plain clothed officer. He must have been tripping if he thought I was going to let him take me down by himself.

I looked back at Chance and the look he gave me reminded me of the look he gave me on the yard, when we were back to back fighting for our lives in that riot. The feeling must have been mutual because at the same time we both pointed our burners in the cop's direction and let him have it.

Boc! Boc! Boc! Boc! Boc! Boc! Boc! Boc! Boc! Boc!

When we pulled our fingers off the triggers we both were standing over the officer with empty chambers.

Uuuuuuurrrrrrrt!

I heard tires screeching and when I looked over the officer's partner was on foot chasing Treasure's car out of the parking lot.

Now how the fuck was I going to get out of there?

TREASURE

They say when your luck is bad, it's bad. Ever since my dad left me my shit's been bad.

I looked in my rearview mirror at the police officer chasing my car and I knew Nu'voe was going to think that I crossed him again by leaving him. *But when bullets and police are involved, it's every man for themselves.* Nu'voe taught me that himself. I thought about going back but the way him and Chance shot up that officer, I knew the whole task force was already on the way.

As I hopped on the freeway, my phone rang. It was Nu'voe calling.

"Hello?"

"What type of shit was that, Treasure?"

"I don't know! That shit happen so fast."

"Why you leave like that!?"

"I don't know bullets started flying everywhere, I was scared. I was scared."

"Never mind, fuck that! Just get to the house and out of that car. I'm sure somebody got a description of it the way you peeled up outta there."

I hung up the phone, drove to the house and got out of the car.

CHAPTER FORTY-FOUR
NU'VOE

I just got off the city bus right in front of the projects. It had been over 20 years since I've rode a city bus, but a nigga didn't have no other choice.

I hopped off the Number 3 bus on Logan Avenue and did my one, two through the projects. The first thing I noticed about my projects was that it had changed. There were gates and barbed wire everywhere. Armed security guards were walking around and cameras could be seen. This shit reminded of where I'd just left.

I shook that thought and memory off and as I pushed through the projects. I saw a few familiar faces and a whole lot of unfamiliar ones. The little snotty nosed boys were now YG's and the pretty little girls were now Ratinahs, Chickenettas, and the homegirls. I noticed one of the YG's standing on the playground. He was patrolling and keeping point.

I approached him, and said, "Aye, lil' homie. Where can I find Babywood at?"

The little homie gripped something in his sweater pocket and shrugged his shoulders as he said, "I don't know. Who is you anyway?"

Down lil' nigga, I thought.

"I'm Nu'voe," I replied and looked right into his eyes.

His eyes bulged out of his head when I said my name. I don't know if it was fear or respect, but the tough, hard role was replaced by an apologetic look. He looked his age.

"You mean Lil' Face's uncle? Nu'voe the O.G.?" he asked.

"Yeah lil' homie," I responded.

Even though I didn't show it, the sound of my nephew's name broke me down.

"Follow me, big homie," the little homie responded and we walked to where Babywood was.

I was in front of the homie giving him the info about everything that had went down. After I was done, the look on Wood's face was shock and amazement. Even though I had gone through the shit, I had to admit that it all sounded like something out of a movie.

Everything got even crazier when he told me about the shit that went down with my nephew and Butch. I only heard about the incident in the hospital, I didn't know that it was my nephew that put him there in the first place. Everything was hitting me at once.

Babywood, always the calm one, rolled two blunts of that good and popped the cork on a fif of Hennessy. The weed calmed my nerves and the drink oozed my chaotic mind as he and I did what we've done for years. We put our heads together and planned, plotted, and strategized.

CHAPTER FORTY-FIVE
TREASURE

I pulled into the garage in case my car was being searched for.

"Fuck I gotta get rid of my baby. I love this fucking car," I sucked my teeth as I briskly walked to the house and inserted the key I'd been given. Once I made it inside I fiddled along the wall until I found the light switch.

Smack!

I stumbled back, totally caught off guard, "What the fu—"

Smack! Smack! Smack!

Finally, I fell to the floor and accepted my ass whooping. Just when I thought I was about to have love made to me, I walked into a fury of punches. *Silly me.*

"You lying bitch! I told ya ass.....stay ...away from..."

Smack! Smack!

I curled up in a fetal position praying that the beating would stop. Smacks turned to punches which led to kicks. I was being beat like I stole a pimp's money.

When it finally stopped, the heavy breathing filled the silent room. The only other thing that could be heard was the light humming of the refrigerator. I was dizzy and completely incoherent.

"Get ya ass up and run the bath water now... hurry the fuck up. Ya stupid ass could have gotten killed for being so fuckin' stupid! Get ya ass in that fucking bath. Now!" I dragged my feet and made my way upstairs and did what I was told. *This shit has to stop.*

CHAPTER FORTY-SIX
*THE HOMIE*CHANCE*

THE HOMIE

Looking at the clock it was almost noon. Chance told us to get dressed because we had a major meeting with some Piru niggas but I couldn't care less. I had something to handle.

I sat on the toilet faking like I was shitting so that they could leave me. I couldn't afford to get caught because I knew Chance would kill me.

Boom! Boom! Boom!

"Yo, Blood! Come on nigga!" Dejuan banged on the door. "Chance is waiting downstairs already."

"I got the shits my nigga. This shit pouring out my ass, Blood." I had to laugh at how that came out. "I'm on house arrest homie, had to be that food from last night."

"Maybe it was that snow bunny's ass all clogged up in ya mouth," he teased.

"Fuck you nigga! Y'all be safe and go ahead."

"A'ight homie."

Finally, I heard the door close and I knew Chance was going to wonder where I was but fuck that nigga. I had something to investigate.

CHANCE

I sat in the driver seat getting some fire ass head from Bianca when I spotted my homies coming out the lobby door. "Baby here they come."

"So what, I can make you cum before they get here," she moaned as she went back to work.

I was parked at the far end of the garage so it would take a minute for them to reach me with how slow they were walking. I gripped a hand full of her pretty ass hair and fucked her mouth. Sure enough, I came before L-God grabbed the door handle. He gave me a smirk as everyone else followed suit.

"Ayo where's—"

"He's on the shitter; nigga got a stomach virus or something like that." KG cut me off reading my mind.

I looked in the rearview mirror and couldn't help but admire my homies, we had our ups and downs but overall it was straight loyalty. It was all real when it came to them. I just couldn't say the same about Nu'voe.

I couldn't help but think about the look on 'Vo's face when we were back to back again. It felt good being that close to my nigga again. The look he gave me when the cop yelled freeze was like a silent bond and we both knew what to do. Through all this I wondered if one day we might be able to put all of this behind us.

THE HOMIE

I caught a cab to the police plaza and was greeted by Officer Sherman. She was cute but a little on the chubby side.

"How may I help you?" she smiled.

"Hi, my name is William Jenkins." I introduced myself. "Umm, I'm looking for my brother that disappeared about a month or so ago."

"Well, have you filled out a missing person's report?" she asked still smiling from ear to ear.

"Nah, I haven't."

"Well, first you have to do that. Then we can go from there." She said explaining the rules to me. I shook my head from side-to-side because I wasn't feeling what she was saying.

"Nah, ma'am I'm from New Jersey and so is my brother. I'm leaving in a few days. Can you please do something?" I pleaded.

I think she could see the desperation written across my face.

"Okay," she sighed. "I could get in trouble for doing this, but I'm willing to help you out."

I described Justin to her down to the freckles on his face. I watched her type into the keyboard. She put her hands over her mouth and gasped for air.

"Is everything alright?" I asked.

She didn't respond, instead she stared at the computer screen and shook her head.

"Ummm, is this him?" she said while turning the computer screen to face me.

My heart dropped to my feet, "Oh shit that's my lil' nigga, I mean brother," I blurted out.

I was looking at a digital picture of him laying on a piece of slab. From what the report said, he suffered from fatal gunshot wounds.

The fucked up thing about it was that in California, when a John Doe is found and no one claims them within ten days they cremate the body.

"I'm so sorry for your loss," she dropped a tear as she spoke.

I didn't respond. I couldn't respond. The only thing and only person on my mind was killing Chance!

CHAPTER FORTY-SEVEN
CHANCE

"Park right here, boo," Bianca said, while pulling her hair into a pony tail.

I maneuvered the caravan and pulled into the spot backwards, facing the exit just in case shit got ugly. Bottom line was that I was still out of bounds and didn't trust none of those niggas.

"Clip up," I said to my homies. On command, each person put one in the head of their weapons. "Keep that chopper ready just in case. KG and L, y'all come wit' me. The rest of y'all stay on point and keep the engine runnin'. If you see anything that don't look right, let ya gun do the talkin'.'"

"Baby, these people. Y'all safe out here trust me." Bianca put her hands on mine. I felt her, but I would be damned if I was going to be caught slipping. *Shit, Nu'voe trusted me, didn't he?*

The look in her eyes was sincere but I lived by the code: No TrustPassing. We made our exit. I tucked my ten millimeter Larken on my waistline and followed behind Bianca. It was hard for me to focus on my surroundings as she swayed that ass from side to side knowing I was watching.

It was like a scene straight out of the movie Friday. Niggas were lifting weights in front of their houses wearing pressed khaki's and Chuck Taylors. These niggas were looking like Tookie Williams with the tennis racket body. All chest and no legs.

My goons and I matched the stares as we entered the small row home. I held the door as my men entered. I threw up a sign to my other goons to signal for them to watch all those niggas. After we entered the house, she led us through the kitchen and into the backyard. We were met by three other dudes and Bianca was the mediator.

"Chance this is Scrap, Mike-Mike, and Redz."

She made her introductions. We all shook hands and went right back to our G-mode. Nobody could be trusted.

Scrap spoke first, and said, "So y'all the Jersey nigga's that's been kickin' up all this dust, huh? What y'all bang, homie?"

He locked eyes with KG. "I'm bangin' that Guerilla Shine, Gangsta Killa Blood," he said while holding his ground and trading the same stare.

"Well we Skyline over here homie," he shot back with a slight attitude.

I gripped the handle and prepared myself before I spoke. "Look we ain't here for all that. We both have a common enemy and that's them Lincoln Park Vista niggas." I paused and looked in everyone's eyes. "Now those niggas crossed me in a major way and in three days the niggas mother will be laid to rest. And in four days his homie Butch will be laid to rest thanks to me and these niggas standing right here."

"Wait, wait," Redz interjected. "You the one that smoked that nigga moms and got Butch in the hospital?"

"Yeah, my nigga. That was us. I can't take all the credit. My niggas been holding me down." I gave credit where it was due. "I need y'all help."

"And how may that be?" Scrap asked.

"I wanna knock this nigga's mother funeral down."

There was a silence as everyone digested what I just said.

"What's in it for us?" Mike-Mike asked while rubbing his chin.

"Well, I got the combination to both of his safes at his Salon and Detail shop. Together there should be at least one fifty in there."

189

L-God's and KG's eyes lit up. Scrap, who seemed to be their leader smiled and extended his hand.

"I like these East Coast niggas. You got a deal and we on deck my nigga. But no funny shit and no faking. We get at these niggas and we get at them hard," he paused, "Say, I didn't even know y'all banged in Jersey."

When he said that I looked at him like he had three heads. "Nigga, we go super hard in Jersey on that Blood shit. Y'all the motherland and all that, but the rules a lil' different back home, my nigga. Y'all niggas B Up," I turned my back to leave. When we exited the stare down outside continued as my homies were ready for whatever. "We Bool homie let's roll."

Twenty Minutes Later

Back at the hotel I could tell Bianca had something on her mind. I mentally prepared myself for what was about to come.

She looked at me. "Chance, are you crazy. Do you really think it's that type of money in there?" she asked with aggression.

"Baby, I know it's close to it in there. I used to watch Babywood and Butch stuff them safes with drug money," I lied just a little bit.

"Chance, you're gonna get me killed!"

"Baby, once this is done I want you to come back to Jersey with me. I got a nice offer on my house and we can move and start a family. You can go to the big city and do ya fashion thing, baby." I had to say it. "I love you, Bianca."

"Are you serious? Do you really mean that shit?" She let the tears roll down her face. "Chance, I love you too," she cried as we held one another and I swear it felt like I was back in the arms of Lanise.

"Are you leaving with me?" I stared deep into her eyes.

"Yes, baby. I'll go back with you and start a new life and a family." Just as we were about to kiss and make love.

Boom! Boom! Boom!

There was a knock at the door. I grabbed my gun and approached the door like the police were knocking. "Who is it?"

"KG, open up son."

When he entered the room he gave me a piece of paper.

"Ayo, Nutty left this note saying he had a family emergency. He packed his shit and rolled out."

CHAPTER FORTY-EIGHT
*BIANCA*TREASURE*

BIANCA

"Call me when you coming back okay baby, I love you," Chance said before we shared an intimate kiss.

Deep inside I knew something had to be done; I fought long and hard with my conscience before I made my decision.

"Love you too, boo."

I waved at Chance as I pulled off.

For the next ten minutes, I drove around aimlessly trying to figure it all out. Before I knew it I was parked out front of Treasure's Salon, *Face 2 Face*. I couldn't help it as the tears streamed down my face. The last time I was there Treasure, Diamond and I had a huge fight. I never had a chance to say goodbye.

Tap! Tap!

I was startled by the knocking on my driver's side window. It was my girl Shante.

I rolled the window down, and asked, "Hey girl, what's going on?"

"My hair, that's what's going on," she pulled her hat off as she spoke. "A bitch need to get right. What, y'all closed down or somethin'?" she asked with both hands on her wide hips. "And why you sittin' here crying ya pretty lil' eyes out?"

"We had some issues that's all; we'll be up and running soon. Plus, you know Diamond passed away so things been a lil' different." I dug in my purse. "Here, take my card. That's my personal contact. I'll do an in-house for you. Just call me."

I tried to get rid of her.

"Okay," she said, getting the hint. "I'll be calling tomorrow. Bye girl!"

She walked off.

Unable to hold it any longer I called Treasure. It went to voice mail so I called right back and just my luck she answered.

"Hello, Bianca?" she said into the phone.

"Hey, ummm, can we talk?" I stumbled over my words.

"Ummm, sure what's good?" she didn't sound like herself.

"Can we meet?"

"Ummmm," she paused. "Not at the moment. What's on ya mind?"

TREASURE

Putting my finger to my lips saying, "Shhhh," I let Bianca speak.

"Look Treasure," she began. "I know shit been kinda crazy between us but I need you to promise me something," she sounded sincere but I had to hold my ground.

"I'm ya girl B, what's up. Talk to me."

"Don't go to Nu'voe's mother's funeral. Promise me you'll find some type of way to get out of going... please." She began to cry. This was good, this was really good.

I had to pry for more.

"What's happening that I shouldn't be there? Nu'voe would be crushed if I didn't support him".

"Just don't go, a lot of people are gonna lose their lives," She cried even harder. "Shit is getting outta hand. I gotta go, just please do what I asked you too." She hung up.

"What did she say?" Carmen asked before I could put my phone down.

"Well, she said not to go to the funeral." I explained. "She said sum'in' about people losing their lives."

"Oh Shit!" she yelled out. "The guy from the restaurant is planning to attack Ms. Johnson's funeral service! Fucking animal! This won't happen if I have anything to do with it!"

The look on her face was of some C.S.I Miami shit.

Boom.

The sound of a door closing echoed through the house.

"You heard that?" I asked.

"Nah, I didn't hear shit. Now lay ya ass on this bed so I can ride ya face before I head to the station."

Bianca

Feeling a little bit better about myself, I went to my mother's to check on her. I hoped Treasure listened to me and didn't go to that service. I couldn't help but think about it. It was one thing to have Chance and his homies, but to have the Skyline niggas helping out, shit was about to go from bad to worst. Bodies would have surely been dropping. I just couldn't wait to get to Jersey with my man.

I hoped Nu'voe burned in hell for what he did to me. But Treasure was my girl, I just hoped it didn't backfire.

CHAPTER FORTY-NINE
SHAVONE

There are some things in life that you're ashamed of and there are some things that just don't bother you. It all started about five years ago. I was speeding in a residential area and the police pulled me over to cite me. When the officer walked up to my driver's side window I noticed that it was a woman. I immediately became embarrassed because I had mentally prepared myself to flirt my way out of the ticket. I had even unbuttoned my blouse so that the officer could get a good look at what I was working with. And she did. A normal ten-minute traffic stop, turned into a thirty-minute conversation. The rest was history.

Officer Sanchez or Carmen and I had been seeing each other ever since. We were scheduled to get married up until a year ago. She started acting funny. A woman can always tell when she's being cheated on and that was exactly what I was feeling.

I received a call from Carmen telling me to leave the house for some bullshit reason. My gut immediately told me she was lying but I did what she wanted me to because Carmen could be real mean sometimes. One time she literally fucked the shit out of me with her baton while I was handcuffed to the bed because I didn't run her bath water.

Anyway, I left the house like she wanted me to but 30 minutes later my jealousy, curiosity and gut feeling made me make a U-turn and head back to the house. When I got there, Carmen's Squad car was in the driveway. I got out my car and went in. The house smelled like another woman. I tip-toed my way through the house following the scent trail of Luscious Cherry Blossom body wash.

At the top of the stairs I could hear the voices of two women. One was Carmen's and the other had me shocked. It was Diamond's friend and co-worker, Treasure! I couldn't believe what I was hearing.

I had to see it with my own two eyes. I crept to the corner of the bathroom door and spied through the crack. The pain I felt when I saw what I saw was the reason why I was pulling into the heart of the Bay Vista projects, notoriously known to be the most dangerous projects in San Diego. But some things needed to be done. I was looking for a man who might not have even been there, and who I really didn't even know.

But that bitch Carmen had fucked over the wrong person.

CHAPTER FIFTY
THE HOMIE

The nigga had me fucked up. I couldn't wait until I had an opportunity to put a cap in this bitch ass nigga Chance. He killed my peoples. He had to reap what he had sown. I hoped the little note I left would buy me sometime. He would've thought I went back to Jersey and then I could catch him slipping and murk his bitch ass. It was all in the element of surprise.

I remember he kept saying something about the Vista. I flagged down a cab. Once inside, the driver greeted me in Arabic.

"Wa-laken,"

Being that my father was Muslim I replied it right back. "Wa-laken-A-Salum Sahiba,"

He cracked a smile.

"You know how to get to the Vista Projects?" I asked him.

"The what?" he twisted up his face.

"You know the Vista Projects-Umm, drugs and girls," I went on to spark, his memory.

His eyes lit up when I said drugs and girls. "My friend-Bay Vista Money-Green-Ohhn, let's go,"

He pulled into the Bay Vista Apartment Projects ten minutes later. I peeled of twenty-five dollars from my wad of money and paid him.

"Be careful Sahaba!" he yelled as he pulled off.

The scenery around me was way different from your average New Jersey Projects. We had Hi-rise buildings while everything there was flat and row houses.

People were staring at me. They could tell I wasn't from there. I stuck out like a sore thumb. The .45 on my hip would've done the talking if a nigga get out of pocket.

There were a group of dudes lifting weights in front of their crib so I figured I could find who I was looking for through them. "Aye. Excuse me," I spoke calm and humble. "Y'all know where I can find Nu'voe?"

"Who you be homie?" a big, bald headed black ass nigga asked me.

"My name is Nutty. I'm looking for Nu'voe and it's about some important shit." I spoke very matter-of-factly but really not wanting to come off the wrong way.

One guy nodded at another then looked back at me. "Follow me, homie."

I followed a brown skin kid into a small apartment. As soon as we walked in it was like we were walking out the back door. When my feet touched the grass, a blunt object slammed across my head.

Wham!

I was wobbly and tried to reach for my gun but the fist coming full speed ahead to my face was all I saw.

Moments Later...

"Wake ya ol' punk ass up," someone with a strong California accent said as they threw water on me. When I came to, I was tied to a chair with my hands bound behind my back.

"Hold up-Hold up! I come in peace!" I shouted as the huge mother fucker I encountered at the door punched me in my ribs.

"Urrr shit!" I took deep breaths hoping they didn't kill me.

"What you want with the big homie? Who the fuck are you, nigga?" someone who I couldn't see asked me.

"I came to talk. I-I-I got some information about his mother," I stuttered, trying to regain my composure.

"Dis nigga lying," the shortest of the group said. "Why you strapped?" he asked holding my gun in the air. Then came another punch to my midsection.

"Ahhh shit... Man I swear I ain't on nothing!" The punches continued. They literally took turns trying all these combos while my body turned to a Ramen noodle soup. I had broken ribs and my right eye was completely closed.

Finally, a voice shouted. "Hold up... Stop... What the fuck is going on back here?"

"This nigga came here looking for you with a SI won't trap," he held the gun up once again. "He walked up after he hopped out a cab and said he looking for you and now look." The short one explained, sounding proud of what he had done to me.

"You must be Nu'voe," I mumbled.

My jaw was so tight I could barely talk. He punched the shit out of me.

He walked over to me and jammed his pistol into my temple.

"You got five minutes, speak." Nu'voe demanded.

I went on to tell him everything. From Chance's plans about shooting up the funeral to meeting with the Piru niggas. I even told him about the shooting in the projects that occurred a few days prior. I fucked up when I mentioned the part about his mother.

"Was you there? Was you there when he killed my mother!" he barked.

I knew I was on borrowed time so I went straight to my Boyz N Da Hood role, "I didn't pull the fucking trigger man, and fuck you!"

As soon as I finished my words he aimed his gun at my right knee.

Boom!

The gun jerked as the flames spit out.

"Ahhh shit-What the fuck man!" I screamed like a bitch from the pain. I had never been shot before and the shit burnt like a motherfucker.

"Nigga if you lying," he put the hot barrel to my forehead burning my skin. "I'ma put a bullet between ya eyes!" he looked around as the crowd stared on. "Lil' homie call ya aunt Tee-Tee, tell her somebody need to be patched up, "With the gun still on my forehead and the smell of burning flesh filling my airway he spoke, "Get this nigga outta here."

CHAPTER FIFTY-ONE
✷CARMEN✷NU'VOE✷

CARMEN

The Chief of Police spoke at the squad briefing. "Today is a very important day for the department, our city, the South East Community and every individual in here. Today we take a step towards ending the war on gangs. Today we take a step towards restoring hope into the inner city. Today, ladies and gentlemen, we take back what's ours. And that's the streets!

"Now, every one of you has your instructions in front of you, along with photos of the two men we are most interested in. You all are proud officers and I know that you will execute this mission with flying colors. But as your Chief of Police, it is my duty to approach this situation with caution, seriousness and the Faith that we will all return back safe. With that being said this meeting is over. Good luck officers; let's go arrest some gang members!"

I hopped in my squad car with my new partner. He was a young white kid and a first year rookie. Ever since my other partner was gunned down, I had been on leave and under investigation. Bureau Policies.

I wouldn't even be going on this sting at all if it was up to the captain. But when I brought the information I had about what was going on, he ended my investigation and allowed me to return to duty. But he also warned me that if the info I provided was false that I might as well pack up my things and move out of town because my days as a San Diego Police Officer would be over.

I hoped to God that Treasure's information was right.

NU'VOE

Treasure was one scandalous bitch! Every time I got a scab to grow over my wounds, she found a way to peel that mother fucker off and pour salt on it! I hope he forgives me when I say this but God really fucked up when he made that thing called LOVE. That shit will have a nigga lose his mind.

Love, no matter how much we try to sugar coat it, is one bad bitch!

Being a real street cat I didn't believe in coincidences. The info I had received from Chance's homeboy had to be 100. It changed everything. I was in the process of revamping my entire game plan for what I just heard.

The more I thought about it, the more I realized that this world we lived in was occupied by nothing but disloyal, dishonest, and untrustworthy mother fuckers.

In two days I was laying to rest the woman who gave me breath. In two days I would be ready for whatever. And in two days, no matter what, my life would never be the same.

CHAPTER FIFTY-TWO
CHANCE

"For Thine is The Kingdom, the Power, and the Glory. Amen," I said a quick prayer before standing to my feet. It was the day I wanted to make sure Nu'voe would never forget. "This is for you, baby," I said as I thought about Lanise and how we first met during my freshman year of high school.

I envisioned her in the courtroom the day I got all that time and the tears ran down her face. I knew she crossed the line, but I still felt that I was the blame. I pushed her beyond her limits and now she was dead over my beef.

I felt Bianca's hands wrap around my waist and her lips pressed against my back. I turned to face her and she kissed my lips before she spoke.

"You promise you're coming back for me?"

Her question caught me off guard.

"Of course I'm coming back, everything is gonna be a'ight, ma. Trust me," I gave her a little assurance.

"Chance, I don't wanna lose you. Promise me you're gonna be okay," she began to cry which was something I was seeing a lot of lately since we found out she was pregnant. I tightly wrapped both my arms around her as her crying had picked up. She completely broke down.

"What's wrong, baby?" I asked trying to see if it was anything else other than me going to put in some work.

"Prom-Promise you won't ever judge me," she cried while she spoke.

"I won't, baby-ever. I promise. Talk to me, baby."

She stared into my eyes and poured her heart out to me. She told everything. She told me about what Nu'voe did to her, about the sexual relationship she had with Treasure and about the fight she had with Diamond on the day that she died.

I couldn't believe the shit Bianca told me. It was just more fuel to kill the nigga so that my wifey could rest in peace and Bianca could bury those demons.

I held her as she drifted off to sleep. Once I made sure she was sleep I slid to my homies room. The stench of weed reeked through the hallway. As I was sliding the key card to open the door, two of the hotel house keepers were coming out fixing their dresses.

I shook my head and laughed knowing my little homies ran through them Mexican bitches.

The sound of Tupac filled the air and that was just what I needed. When I looked around KG, L-God, and Dejuan were loading up weapons, preparing for war. Rajohn passed me a blunt while I bopped my head to one of my favorite Pac songs.

"Bet you mutha-fuckas die when we ride on our enemies."

"Aye, Chance. We need to get some whips right now so we can have them already rigged up before that time come. We getting close." KG said while loading AK shells in the chopper.

"Yeah, you right," I had to agree. "Come on." Dejuan, KG, and I exited the room while L-God continued to load up.

We rode in the caravan to an apartment complex that was a couple blocks away.

"Right thurr," KG said as he spotted two easy vehicles to get. A tan Dodge Intrepid parked next to a Buick Regal. "Pull in front."

Quickly, Dejuan and I hopped out with our pullies and slim jims in hand. The few people who were outside didn't care what was going on. Like true Jersey Niggas, we were in and out in seconds. I popped the Regal's steering column and snatched the ignition out with the pully. A few slugs and voila. I looked over and Dejuan was on some Cleo shit trying to find a CD to listen to.

"Let's go!" I shouted, smashing the gas and spinning tires all the way out the parking lot.

****

Back at the hotel room we all sat staring at one another. The room was tense and we all knew what had to be done.

"Bianca, here is the combination to the safes and keys to the front doors of both the rim and beauty spot. You have enough time to go there, get the money, drop it off to ya people and have ya ass at that airport when we get there." I paused to look around. "We all have E-tickets waiting at Delta Airlines. Our flight leaves at 3:15pm. Whoever isn't there must be dead because no one leaves a man alive in battle. Clip up!"

Vrrr! Vrrr!

I was interrupted by the vibration of my phone. "Hello."

"They just started pulling up to the funeral home."

Click!

That was what I needed to hear.

"Ayo, the Skyline niggas are in position. Two in the Regal, three in the Intrepid. I remember the way and y'all know I got the wheel." We all stood up and shook hands and hugged as they made their exit.

I turned to face Bianca who was crying again.

"I love you; baby and I'll see you at the airport."

"I'm waiting on you baby, I'm waiting," she cried.

We made sure nobody left anything behind before we left the rooms.

It's on now. I walked her to her car and kissed her deeply. As our lips parted, I spoke.

"He will pay for what he did to you, I Promise." before she could utter a word I stepped off and made my way to the Regal. I brought the engine to life and revved the dual exhaust.

She ran back to me and kissed me once more. "Love you, baby." I kissed her forehead and spun tires out the parking lot.

CHAPTER FIFTY-THREE
*NU'VOE*BIANCA*CHANCE*

NU'VOE

I didn't know how to explain what I was feeling or what I was about to do. I was supposed to be burying my mother but I was getting ready to go to war against the nigga who killed her. I hoped the man upstairs and my mom forgave me because I was going all in!

I got a phone call. I looked at my phone and the number that flashed on the screen let me know what time it was. When I read the message that followed the number it confirmed what I already knew. It was time to get it cracking!

I immediately hopped out of my seat while the preacher was in the middle of the eulogy and gracing my mom. To everybody there, it looked like I couldn't handle the service, but to my niggas, it meant game time.

By the time I got outside the church, Chance and his crew were bending the block. That's when everything hit slow motion.

I'm not the church type of person, but I do believe in the man upstairs and when I saw those cars bending the block, the spirit inside of me stirred. It felt like my mom and my nephew were right by my side talking to me. They were telling me to get out of there.

The type of feeling I had was the type you get at the bottom of your stomach when you know bad was going to happen. Even though I knew Chance was coming to shoot up mom's funeral, the respect for the game that I have wouldn't let me believe it. But the first four shots and Chance's homeboy's head opening up like a cantaloupe changed my beliefs. I had instructed the homies to wait on my call, but with these niggas getting at us the way they did, all bets were off. The war had officially started.

My instincts kicked in and I reached for my pistol on my hip. It was a fo-nickel, 1911 series equipped with an extended clip, holding 25My homies we in the clip and one in the chamber. The stainless steel and beam was extra.

The sounds and scene around me reminded me of the movie, "Jar head". Hot ones and guns busting everywhere. The shit was unbelievable.

My mind had blanked out and my eyes saw red. I gripped my burner and squeezed.

Pop! Pop! Pop! Pop! Pop! Pop! Pop! Pop! Pop!

One of the cars in Chance's entourage swerved and crashed into a limo. Three of the shots I fired penetrated the drivers face.

When I looked to my right did I see my little homie's head separate from his body? He had caught a dome shot!

After seeing the homie get his noodles blown I flew down the stairs, ran up to the champagne colored Cutlass and emptied my clip into the passenger side window.

Pop! Pop! Pop! Pop! Pop! Pop!

Click! Click!

Realizing I was out of bullets, I took a peek into the Cutlass.

"What the fuck?!" Inside the Cutlass was a nigga from Skyline Piru that I had beef with back in the day. "What he doin' shootin' up my mom's funeral?" Right then I knew Chance had linked up with the Skyline's to knock me and the homies off all at once. Then I felt a sharp, burning pain. I was hit in the arm with something phat!

CHANCE

"Run nigga, run!" I yelled out loud as I brought the car to a stop. "Okay, fuck this handgun! It's time to go rapid on dey ass!" I exited the car and took cover.

For some reason it seemed like the niggas were expecting us.

I raised my Altra Tech with a thirty-two round clip, aimed at my target and went to work.

Blaat! Blaat! Blaat!

My first shot took a nigga out that was standing close to Nu'voe. Then on cue the hunter green F-150 with the Skyline homies in it came flying down the one way. I opened fire again, giving them cover.

"Yo, Chance!"

I turned around to see my nigga Dejuan coughing up blood. "Nah! Not my nigga!" I grabbed the AR-15 that laid next to him, tossed my tech around my neck and started squeezing.

"Damn, it's the police?"

BIANCA

My first stop was the shop, *Face 2 Face*. After a short drive I parked around back and using my key I opened the back safety door. Within seconds I had disarmed the ADT alarm system and headed to Treasure's office.

Looking around, images of Diamond, Treasure and the girls flashed through my mind.

"Shake that shit off B, focus!" I said out loud.

I knelt down to be eye-level with the safe and punched in the code Chance gave me. The door latch popped open. When I opened it up all the way, looking back at me were stacks of green faces. Wasting no time, I opened my YSL purse and filled it up. It had to be about 40 to 70 thousand dollars in there. Quickly, I got to my feet and made my exit.

20 Minutes Later

This is the first time I've ever seen the Detail and Rim shop empty like this. I was glad it was like that though because I was there to clean up. Doing the same thing I did at the other shop I filled up my bag. There was more money in that safe so I couldn't fit it all, but what I did grab was definitely gonna make my man happy. It was so smart of Chance to change the locks so that Babywood couldn't get in and take the money out he had dropped off earlier that week.

I was supposed to drop that money off to the east side homies but when that much money is in your hands it does something crazy to you. You lose all sense of normal thinking.

Fuck that loyalty shit. The nigga that was laying pipe the right way was the only one I was loyal to. So I decided to meet my man at the funeral with the money and my strap. I was going to hold him down like a real Cali bitch.

NU'VOE

The hot one that hit me in the arm spun me around and dropped me where I stood. They say when you're on your way to meet the man upstairs you see a bright ass light and your entire life flashes before your eyes. I don't know about any light, but I sure as hell saw my life flash before my eyes.

NO TRUSTPASSING

I was ten years old and my older relative had told me a secret. He made me promise not to tell anybody. I agreed, but when my aunt asked me about what happened, I told her. After that, my relative didn't tell me anything else for five years and I learned a valuable lesson. Your word is all you got.

If Treasure and Chance would have kept their word none of this would have happened. One TRUST-PASS can do a whole lot of damage.

"Get up Unk! Get up!" I swore I could hear my nephew's voice.

Then I heard screams from the police. When I got to my feet the first thing I saw was a black on black Buick Regal barreling down on me. With a hole in my left arm and bleeding like a stuck pig, I reached to the small of my back with my right hand. There was no way I was going to get to my pistol in time. I closed my eyes and waited for the impact.

Uuuuurrrrrttttttt...

CHANCE

Looking at Nu'voe, I could have easily run his ass over or blew his brains out. I already got him in the arm.

My homies were dead and it was time to end it all! I brought the car to a complete stop, hopped out and aimed the .44 bulldog at his head.

"Chance! Come on yo! What the fuck you doin'?" KG was screaming at me.

"Keep it movin'. What's poppin' now, nigga?" I yelled as Nu'voe and I locked eyes. "This shit ends here nigga!"

"Police, freeze! Get down!"

211

CHAPTER FIFTY-FOUR
*OFFICERS*CARMEN*NU'VOE*CHANCE*

CARMEN

"We're in position, give us the green light!" Another officer's voice barked through the walkie-talkie. "I can't believe these mutha-fuckas are really doing this."

I know the streets can be a vicious place and rules change, but shooting up a funeral was crazy. As soon as the Buick Regal followed by the Dodge Sedan surfaced, I knew from all my years of training that something bad was about to happen.

Looking through my binoculars I spotted an AK 47 German issue assault rifle and knew right then it would be a gun fight. I hoped my fellow officers were ready because those assholes were definitely taking it to the streets. I grabbed my walkie talkie and yelled into it.

"Take 'em out now! Now!"

Boc! Boc! Boc!

"It's a fucking warzone out here!" I yelled in my walkie talkie. I couldn't believe all the firepower those street punks had access to.

I knelt down behind my squad car hoping to gain some type of cover, but those fucking AK 47's was tearing holes in everything that they hit. Looking to my right I saw my colleague, Officer Jones aiming his infrared beam on Nu'voe's head. But I couldn't let another cop have the pleasure of killing either one of these assholes.

I aimed my Glock 9 at my longtime friend, closed my right eye and planted two slugs in his neck.

Boc! Boc!

As fast as the gun jerked in my grip, he was dead. Nu'voe would have never seen that coming. But this was personal. This was for Treasure.

Seeing that I was low on ammo for my Glock I went to my ankle holster and pulled my .10 mm sidearm. I put another clip in my Glock and aimed into the crowd of gangbangers.

Not caring who I hit, I let both guns rip through the air.

Boc! Boc! Boom! Boom! Boom! Boc! Boc! Boc!

I dipped back behind my car, but then the glass from the front window burst over top of me.

Baka! Baka! Baka! Baka!

I yelled into my walkie talkie again. "Need assistance! I repeat, need assistance!"

"I'm hit! I'm hit! Ahhr!" I heard through all the commotion. It was Officer Brooks and to think today was her day off.

"Officer down! Officer down!" I yelled into the receiver before hearing the sound of tires screeching.

Urrrrrrrr!

The Buick Regal was swerving, trying get away. There were dead bodies sprawled all over the place. Some in uniform and some in civilian clothing with big guns lying next to them. The sad part was the elderly people who lay injured on the steps of the funeral home and on-lookers who fell victim to stray bullets.

When I turned my attention behind me, I noticed two men standing in the street with their guns pointed at each other. From where I stood, I couldn't tell exactly who they were. With both weapons drawn out in front of me, I approached.

As I got closer I noticed it was the two men I had been looking for, Nu'voe and Chance. It was a shame they were both going to die by my hands. Treasure would never leave me again!

With my finger wrapped around the trigger of both guns, I yelled out. "Drop ya weapons!" but they didn't budge.

"Chaaaaaannnnccceee, baby Noooooooooo!" I heard a female's voice yell out. When I looked there was a beautiful woman running full speed. And Treasure was right behind her.

Oh hell no, I thought when I saw her running. I was instantly infuriated. *She tryna save this nigga? She will not leave me... fuck that, she will... Not... Leave... me!*

"Drop your weapons!" I yelled out once more, this time eager to end both of their lives. Unexpectedly, someone came from behind me and opened fire.

Boc! Boc! Boc! Boc!

"Catch'em!" I yelled to Officer Cantose who was right behind me.

It boiled down to them or me.

With every step Treasure took, the tears in her eyes and the emotions she felt for that man were written all over her face. It finally hit me. I couldn't beat Nu'voe, she would never love me the way she loved him. I couldn't compete. And I wouldn't compete. Treasure was mine!

With hatred, betrayal, and jealousy in my heart, I had to eliminate my competition. Chance and Nu'voe.

Sirens blared coming from afar and it was my window to have my dirty deeds unnoticed. I was the only cop on the scene and could tell my boss anything.

"I Love you, Treasure. I'm doing this for you!"

Boom! Boc! Boom! Boom! Boc! Boc!

NO TRUSTPASSING

NU'VOE

No matter who you are or where you are, real will always recognize real. With pistols in our hands, our eyes locked on each-other, and our homies dying at our feet, the feeling was mutual.

The shit had to end here.

"Nu'voe! Nu'voe!" Somebody was yelling my name.

Boc! Boc! Boc! Boc! Boc!

Shots rang out. When I turned to look at who was calling me, I saw Babywood running with a Chop Suey in his hand. I felt like I was in Vietnam. Everything went silently black! My body got hot, cold, and then numb. I had never seen so much blood in my life. Death was knocking at my door. Death was calling my phone. Death was bringing me home!

It was unbelievable. With everything going on, the one thing that surfaced to my mind was my baby and with my last breath I called out her name.

"Treasure!"

CHANCE

Visions of me and Nu'voe on the yard together clouded my mind. We were smoking K-2 late night in the cell, emailing each other's bitches for one another when we ran out of minutes or words to send were all I could think of at that moment. Just the memory of me holding my nigga down and him holding me down. I struggled to pull the trigger.

Then it hit me.

Boc! Boc! Boc!

I felt the same feeling I felt back in 2003 when I got hit up! Damn, he pulled the trigger and as I fell on my side all I heard was my name being called.

"Chance! Chance! Baby noooooooooooo!"

And my last thoughts were of Bianca. Then I saw my father behind her.

CHAPTER FIFTY-FIVE
TREASURE

The last nine months of my life had been filled with nothing but abuse and drama. Carmen's been another person lately and it's like no matter what I do she's never happy. I try to cook and she doesn't want to eat. I clean up and she throws shit around. I try to make love and she wants to fight.

About a month or so ago she went through my closet and found a picture I had of Nu'voe and Chance together when they were locked up. She came to my place of business and embarrassed me. Then she waited until I got home and beat me unconscious.

It got to the point where I didn't even go out anymore. My eyes were always puffy from crying or evidence of another beating. It was 8:10 a.m. and I was cussing out God for waking me up.

I didn't have any friends. Bianca was a model and she lived in Lajolla somewhere. She somehow came up on a big piece of money. But I was totally broke. All of my safes at the shops had been hit and Nu'voe didn't leave me with nothing. To make matters worse, I picked up a slight cocaine habit fucking with Carmen. It was only to ease my stress and to help me please myself because a bitch hadn't been getting any loving.

It was time for a bump while I was bullshitting around and decided to watch TV. I hit the power control to my 64-inch flat screen and my girl Lisa Lake was on Channel 7 live news. When I went to the closet to get my stash that's when I heard it.

"Live from M.C.C. The San Diego holding facility for Federal Prisoners where two inmates who were listed to be in comas have escaped."

I dropped the remote and put both of my hands over my mouth when Nu'voe's and Chance's faces popped up on the screen.

"Ohhh shit," were the only words I could say. I turned up the volume as the reporter went on about the story.

"These are the faces of a Mr. Nu'vaar Du'voe, a San Diego native and known affiliate to the Lincoln Park Blood Gang and a Mr. Demarcus Hood, a New Jersey Native also connected to the Blood Street gang in New Jersey.

"Apparently, the two men somehow conspired to escape after a gruesome standoff with the S.D.P.D. We have no leads, no clues, and no connecting suspects at this time. Several guards are being questioned in connection to this escape. If you have any leads, please don't hesitate to call 1-800-ILL-TELL. Once again these men are very dangerous and may be armed..." The reporter paused for a second.

"Wait, this just in. These two men were cellmates at USP Leavenworth about a year ago. It is highly likely that these two are together and looking to flee the country. They were facing several murder charges and weapon possession charges as well. Once again, look at the faces of these two men and please be careful citizens of California and all across the world. This is Lisa Lake back to you Jim."

"Ooooh shit... No... No... No... There out... Oh My God he's gonna come after Me!" I said out loud. Then I heard my door slam. "Oh Nooooooo!"

NO TRUSTPASSING

REVENGE
OFFICER GIBSON

"Job well done boys!" I slapped hands with the mastermind and Assistant Warden of M.C.C. Federal Holdover. He, his Lieutenant and I were Frat buddies back in the day at S.D.S.U.

"Your welcome buddy. So, let me ask you what are you gonna do with these assholes? I mean look at them, they're damn near dead." A.W. Jenkins laughed while he counted his $25,000 share from the escape.

I sat and listened while rubbing the scar on the left side of my jaw from the gunshot wound. Most people thought it was a dimple, but it was far from that. The .40 caliber bullet fractured my jaw line and broke ten teeth. I wore dentures to cover up what happened to me and I'm running off one kidney with two bullets still stuck in my abdomen.

Staring at Chance and Nu'voe's unconscious bodies I couldn't help the chills that ran down my spine thinking back to that night at Lucy's. They tried to take me out, end my life, and ruin my family. But I survived. After eight long months of therapy, I have a vendetta against my bosses. Not the bosses of the force, but the bosses of the underworld, Pierre and Skinny Tony.

I took hits for hire as a sice hustle to make some extra money. That night at Lucy's I was following a target and these assholes fucked it up. The person I was ordered to kill got away and testified against fifteen members of my crew and it was their entire fault!

I watched my wife get raped and beaten. And being that I could barely walk to protect my damn self, my face was used as a human ashtray for missing my mark. So not only will Skinny Tony and Pierre pay, but Chance and Nu'voe will pay as well.

I hired two nurses to work around the clock to bring my boys back to life and when they come back to they will work for me. If they want their lives back, I can make it happen. Not only did Carmen violate Penal Code Section 8987 by having sexual relations with an informant, but I have all the evidence. I had the gun that took the life of Nu'voe's nephew, the murder weapons used at the funeral home shooting which took the lives of seven officers, and personal wire taps I placed in Carmen's home on nights we made love.

I never trusted that bitch. She knew I was on to her so she left me for dead that night in the parking lot.

After these assholes complete the job at hand I'll personally deliver Treasure to them on a platter along with Carmen as a side dish.

Beep! Beep! Beep!

"Sir, they're breathing on their own." Nurse Betty said with a smile on her face while rubbing the boys' hands.

"Yeah, that's right, fight for ya lives. Your gonna need it."

To Be Continued...
No TrustPassing Part 2
Coming Soon

Deception

I'm all around you... Everywhere you turn I'm there just waiting for you to slip and let me in.

I'm the hand you just shook and that door you just opened.

I'm the woman lying in bed next to you, look at the signs and you'll see. I'm the reason your right hand man is plotting on you.

I'm the reason why you're gonna be the victim of a robbery, kidnapping and worst of all murder.

Oh let me guess, you still don't know who I am, you trusted me too huh... I done broke down my crews with AIDS.

I'm the reason niggas get on the stand and tell the Feds all they wanna hear. And when me and my boys lust, hate, envy, jealousy, gossip, evil, and lies come through... Oh y'all really in for it then.

You think you're safe... You really think we're friends huh....

Why is it people always see a stray dog roaming the streets, take them in, and offer them food and then get mad when you get BIT!?

NIGGA, I was a stray dog when you met me, that's why you got bit.

Use ya eyes and never ignore the signs, in this game you have no LOVE, LOYALTY, TRUST, HONOR, RESPECT ... So wise up and STOP TRUST PASSING!

By Hood

Established in 2012 Legit Styles Concierge is the "right connection" to meet your needs; whether business, personal, social and beyond. Everyone has a loved one that is distant and we are here to unlock your mind with our fingertips. We provide freedom from the inside by taking pride in connecting you to the outside world with our services.

-- Local numbers
-- Social Media accounts (Hi5, Tagged, FB, IG etc.)
-- Book/Magazine orders
-- Gift Services

Would you like to be an author?
We are currently accepting submissions.
Please email or mail your complete manuscript or for more info contact us:

Legit Styles Concierge
16501 Shady Grove Rd Suite #7562
Gaithersburg, MD 20898

For federal inmates email us: info@legit-Styles.com
Visit us at: www.Legit-Styles.com

Book Order Form
Legit Styles Publishing
16501 Shady Grove Rd Suite #7562
Gaithersburg, MD 20898

Name: _____   Inmate ID: _____

Address: _____

City/State: _____

QUANTITY	TITLES/AUTHORS	PRICE	TOTAL
	KINGPIN, Byron Grey	15.00	
	The Wall Season 1, Don Twan	15.00	
	Confessions of A Cheating Heart, Donnie Ru and Don Twan	15.00	
	No TrustPassing, Hood & Face 1	15.00	
	Pay The Cost, Michael "Blue" Branch	15.00	
	A.B.C.G. (Anybody Can Get it) DeSean Gardner	15.00	
	Small Town Cemetery DeSean Gardner	15.00	
	COMING SOON!!		
	KingPin 2, Byron Grey		
	The Wall 2, Don Twan		
	No TrustPassing 2, Hood and Face 1		
	The Initial Investigation, Byron Grey		
	Murderland, Byron Grey		

Sub Total $_____ Shipping $_____ Total Enclosed $_____

Shipping & Handling (Via US media Mail) $ 3.95 1-2 book(s), $ 7.95 3-4 books, 4 books or more free shipping.

FORMS OF ACCEPTED PAYMENTS:

Certified or government issued checks and money orders, all mail in orders take 5-7 business days to be delivered. Books can be purchased by credit card at 1-800-986-0000 or on our website at www.legitstylespublishing.com. Incarcerated readers receive 25% discount. Please pay $11.25 and apply the same shipping terms as stated above.

www.ingramcontent.com/pod-product-compliance
Lightning Source LLC
Chambersburg PA
CBHW031154270326
41931CB00006B/270